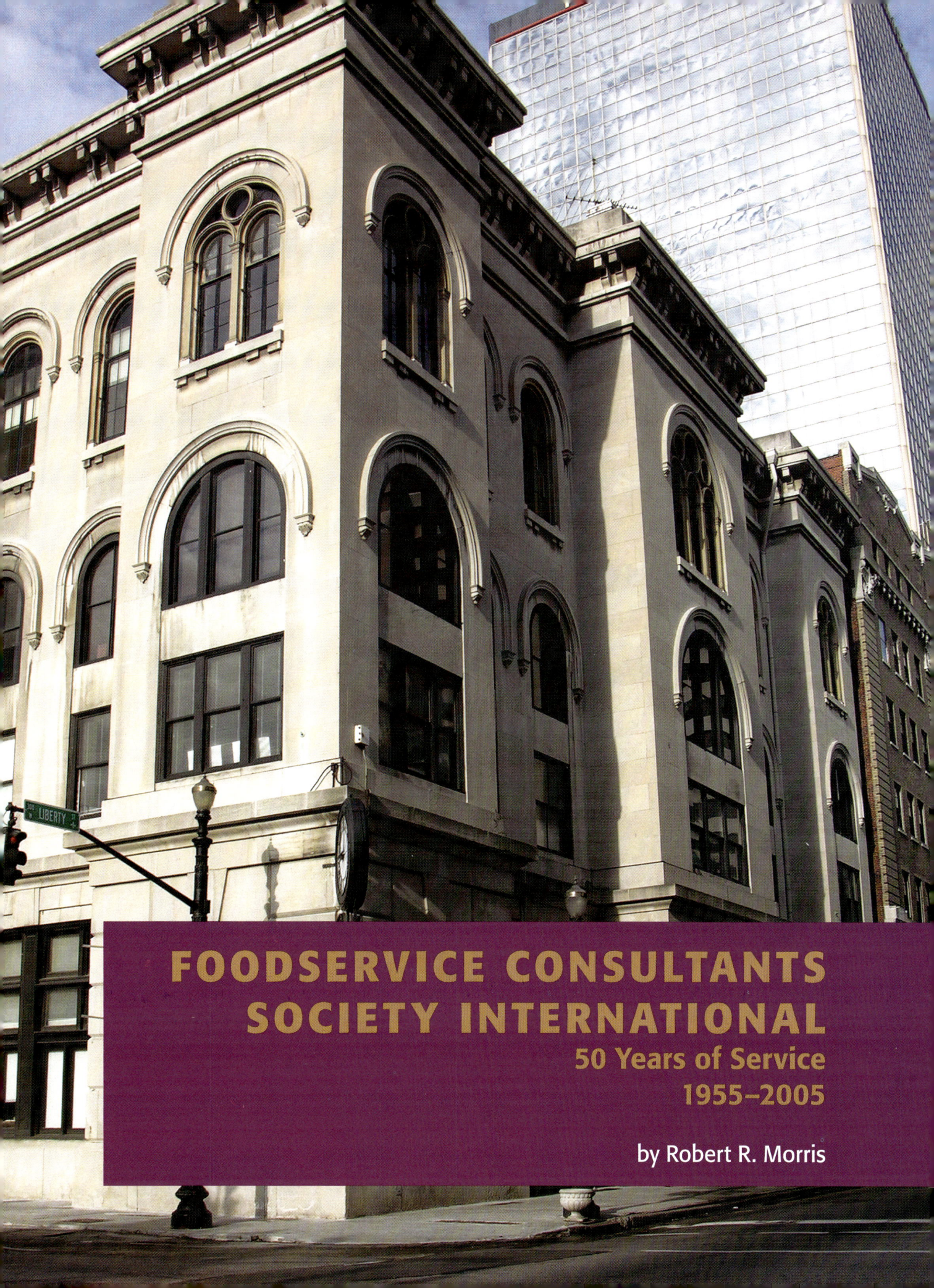

FOODSERVICE CONSULTANTS SOCIETY INTERNATIONAL
50 Years of Service
1955–2005

by Robert R. Morris

FOODSERVICE CONSULTANTS SOCIETY INTERNATIONAL
50 YEARS OF SERVICE
1955–2005

Author, Additional Photography
Robert R. Morris
Robert R. Morris Associates, Inc.
rrminc@comcast.net

THE
DONNING COMPANY
PUBLISHERS

Copyright © 2005
Foodservice Consultants Society International
304 West Liberty Street, Suite 201
Louisville, KY 40202
502-583-3783
www.fcsi.org

All rights reserved. No part of this book may be reproduced in any form or by any means, electronic, mechanical, photocopying and recording or otherwise without prior permission of FCSI.

The Donning Company Publishers
Steve Mull, *General Manager*
Barbara B. Buchanan, *Office Manager*
Lisa Rule and Richard A. Horwege, *Editors*
Andrea Eisenberger, *Graphic Designer*
Stephanie Bass, *Imaging Artist*
Mary Ellen Wheeler, *Proofreader*
Cindy Smith, *Project Research Coordinator*
Scott Rule, *Director of Marketing*
Stephanie Linneman, *Marketing Coordinator*

Ed Williams, *Project Director*

Library of Congress Cataloging-in-Publication Data

Morris, Robert R., 1946–
   Foodservice Consultants Society International 50 years of service, 1955–2005 / author, additional photography, Robert R. Morris.
      p.   cm.
   ISBN 1-57864-320-1 (hard cover : alk. paper)
  1. Food service management—History. 2. Foodservice Consultants Society International—History. I. Foodservice Consultants Society International. II. Title.
TX911.3.M27M683 2005
647.95'068—dc22

2005018405

Printed in the USA at Walsworth Publishing Company

Foodservice Consultants Society International would like to thank the following companies and individuals for their financial contribution to this anniversary book project:

Benefactor ($1,000 or more)
Clevenger Associates

Sponsor ($500–$999)
Kochman Consultants, Ltd.
RJS Associates
Salvatore N. Romano, FFCSI (PP)

Patron ($250–$499)
William H. Bender, FCSI
William J. Caruso, FFCSI, ISHC
Food Systems Consulting Inc.
Theodore Barber & Company
Leif Torné, FCSI
Van Velzen + Radchenko Design Ltd.

Supporter ($100–$249)
Arlene Spiegel & Associates
James Barrett, FCSI
Beer Associates
James C. Camacho, FCSI
Carol NL Chia
James G. Cosper, FCSI
David L. Drain
FRANZEN Beratung, Moderation & Gutachten
Stanley Gatland, FCSI
JM Consulting
Joseph Baum & Michael Whiteman Company
Takao Minami, FCSI
Michael H. Redlin, FCSI
Roger Kruse Associates
Tim Smallwood, FCSI
Howard "Kamau" Stanford, FCSI
Jay Treadwell, FCSI

Friend (up to $99)
Don J. Kohne, FCSI
Robert Wm. Whitney, FCSI (EM)
Ed Norman, FCSI

Table of Contents

7	Mission Statement
9	Letter from the President
11	Letter from the Executive Vice President
13	In 1955:
15	Introduction
16	*Chapter 1* AT THE BEGINNING
40	*Chapter 2* SLOW YET STEADY
60	*Chapter 3* A UNIFIED FRONT
86	*Chapter 4* WORLDWIDE PRESENCE
114	*Chapter 5* FCSI AT FIFTY
136	About the Author

Al Da Costa presents superstar chef Emeril Lagasse with the 2003 Trendsetter Award in New Orleans.

Above:
Bill Eaton and Mary Gratzer

Left:
Ken Schwartz

MISSION STATEMENT

To promote professionalism in foodservice and hospitality consulting while returning maximum benefits to all members.

The Foodservice Consultants Society International (FCSI) serves specialists and practitioners in layout and design, planning, research, training, technology, operations, and management. FCSI is the only such consulting Society in the world, with more than 1,100 members in 40 countries.

Foodservice consultants provide valuable professional services to foodservice and hospitality businesses that are:

- Considering the feasibility of a new project
- Creating a new concept
- Striving to reduce costs, increase efficiency, or improve quality
- Building or renovating their facility
- Considering new equipment or technology

These are merely examples from an extensive list of services FCSI members can provide to their clients.

ACKNOWLEDGMENTS

FCSI would like to thank the following members for reviewing the text prior to publication.

Ira Beer, FFCSI	Russ Nickel, FFCSI Emeritus
Bruno Brivio, FFCSI Emeritus	John Radchenko, FCSI
Hugh Cade, FFCSI	Sal Romano, FFCSI
Tom Costello, FFCSI	Bob Schmid, FCSI Emeritus
Sam Crabtree, FFCSI Emeritus	Howard Stanford, FCSI
Nicholas Elshof, FFCSI Emeritus	Leif Torné, FCSI
John Fellers, FFCSI Emeritus	Ken Winch, FCSI
Scott Legge, FCSI	

Then-FCSI Europe chair Ken Winch (right) shakes hands with Pierre Devaux in January 2000 at the signing of the affiliation agreement creating FCSI France. Gerhard Franzen (center) represented FCSI Germany during the signing.

Above:
Intense conversations during a leadership summit meeting held before the 2002 conference in Barcelona.

Left:
Al Da Costa (right) thanks Rudy Miick as he completes his term as chair of the FCSI North American Division in 2003.

Dear FCSI Member and Friend,

I am pleased and honored to present to you this book detailing the wonderful history of the Foodservice Consultants Society International. Our organization is fifty years old in 2005, and throughout those decades, we have been extremely fortunate to have many dedicated and devoted members who have worked tirelessly to promote and improve our organization.

At the initial meeting held in Chicago in 1955 were a tiny handful of foodservice consultants who shared similar interests and sought professional interaction. They formed an organization, which has evolved over the ensuing decades in response to the changing needs of the members and the changing nature of the marketplace.

Our members formed goals, sought a wider audience, and embraced an international community of professionals, all committed to providing excellence in foodservice consulting services.

We have seen the organization become a recognized international leader providing services, education, and a prominent voice in what has become a respected and recognized profession.

Those are impressive accomplishments, and we all should pause to appreciate them and to lend our voices in thanks to those who have brought about this wonderful association.

I hope you enjoy reading this book as much as I have. Happy 50th anniversary to you and all the members and friends of FCSI.

Sincerely,

Kenneth Winch,
President

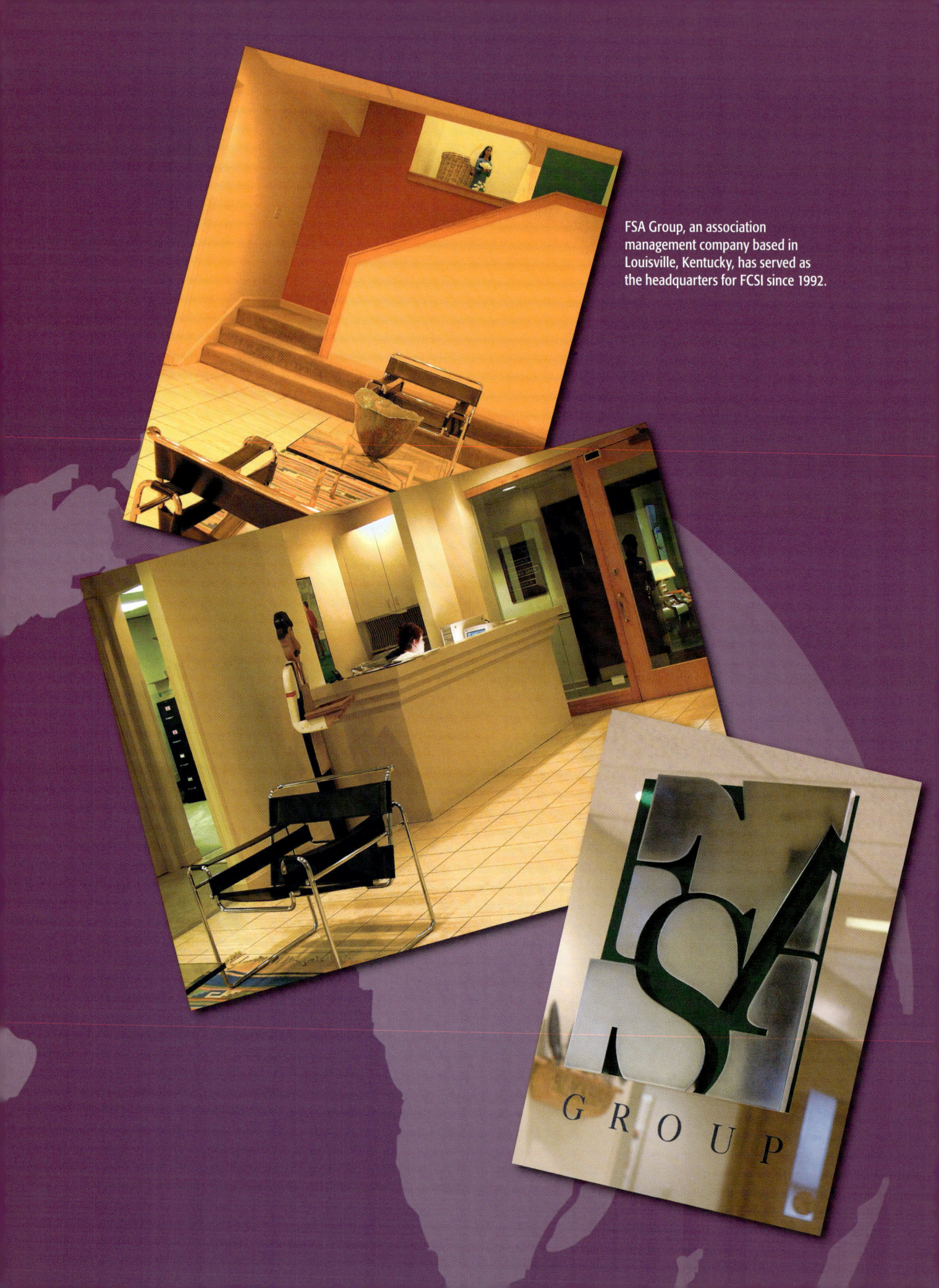

FSA Group, an association management company based in Louisville, Kentucky, has served as the headquarters for FCSI since 1992.

Dear Loyal Friend,

For most of us who work in the foodservice industry, FCSI is the clear leader in professionalism and service to its members. That has been brought about by the deep desire of our members for a Society which is responsive to their needs and agile enough to adapt to continuous changes in technology and information in the foodservice industry.

FCSI has always "been there" to help the members. Publications, conferences, our website, newsletters, phone support, and educational programs all combine to provide our members with a high degree of current, useful, proactive information. That enables everyone to do their job better, which improves the entire industry.

I am proud to join you in celebrating our 50th anniversary. Our organization is now considered the touchstone of excellence for professionals working in foodservice. However, we are young enough so that many of our members have a direct connection to the events and the visionaries who found the need for this organization and worked zealously to establish it.

Indeed, FCSI has changed in many ways since the early years. However one thing has never changed—our determination to provide the highest quality, most professional services to all our members and the industry. We believe we have succeeded in that task. That, too, is something to celebrate.

As you read through the pages of this book, no doubt you will see the panorama of members who have made a difference. Our history now becomes our legacy. None of it could have been attained without you. Please join me in honoring those who have made FCSI such a success. Thank you for your role in our history!

Sincerely,

David Drain,
Executive Vice President

Right:
Ken Winch (left) and George Zawacki

Below:
David Drain, FCSI Executive Vice President

IN 1955:

- Sir Winston Churchill, Britain's legendary wartime Prime Minister, resigned at the age of 80...

- U.S. President Dwight Eisenhower suffered a heart attack, but recuperated quickly and resumed his work...

- Argentina's President Juan Peron was removed from office by a military coup...

- Montgomery, Alabama seamstress Rosa Parks refused to give up her seat on a bus, sparking a boycott which led to the Civil Rights Movement...

- Nobel Prize winners Albert Einstein and Sir Alexander Fleming both passed away...

- Italy, West Germany, and France established the European Union...

- King Norodom Sihanouk of Cambodia abdicated the throne in favor of his father, King Norodom Suramarit...

- The first U.S. "Theme Park," Disneyland, opened on a 22-acre site in Anaheim, California...

- The "Warsaw Pact," a military alliance of the Soviet Union and eastern European nations, was begun as a counter to the North Atlantic Treaty Organization (NATO)...

- The polio vaccine developed by American researcher Dr. Jonas Salk was approved for use...

- Indonesian President Sukarno held a conference of regional Asian nations formerly colonized by the European powers to plan the post-colonial era...

- **...On May 11, 1955, the Foodservice Consultants Society International's ancestor organization, the Food Facilities Engineering Society (FFES) was founded in Chicago by thirteen visionaries intent on professionalizing their work...**

Vince Antoniello (left) and John Cini

Right:
John Radchenko, member of both the Worldwide and North American Boards, during the 2004 Asia Pacific conference in Singapore

Below:
Members discuss burning issues during the FCSI "Chat Room" in Barcelona in 2002.

INTRODUCTION

The Foodservice Consultants Society International traces its founding to the mid-1950s. The profession and its organization grew out of the widespread cultural and social changes that swept over North America following the Second World War. As the association grew, its influence broadened and gained enthusiastic members in Europe, then Asia and across the globe.

The postwar revolution in foodservice started, matured and grew, and eventually adopted an international view. It has been transformed into a profession that benefits from a global outreach and sharing of ideas, techniques, and approaches.

The pioneers who worked so hard to establish the European chapter often toiled amidst traditional American insularism. Yet, despite those drawbacks, they realized there was much to be learned from their American colleagues and much that Americans could learn from them. Today, the international spirit of FCSI provides intellectual stimulus for ideas which benefit members and the general public irrespective of the oceans dividing them.

Flexibility, professionalism, education, and adaptability are the hallmarks of a flourishing and healthy association. FCSI has attained that maturity and today stands as a benchmark for others to measure by in an international marketplace.

To accomplish this in five decades is not only unusual; it is a tribute to the people who founded the Society as well as those who work so very hard for its current well-being. To all the members and friends of FCSI—we dedicate this book.

The realization of this book started with a dream envisioned by the FCSI Worldwide Board together with Executive Vice President David Drain. This history has been compiled using the organization's considerable documentation and archives and has been enhanced by hours of interviews with key members from various FCSI and predecessor eras.

David Drain and his staff at FCSI headquarters in Louisville, Kentucky, were very organized and well prepared, helping the author conduct research while on-site.

Because a good portion of this history is gleaned from personal recollections often fogged in the mist of time, independent confirmation of the facts is difficult or at times impossible. However, everything presented here is done with the belief that we have achieved the greatest accuracy possible.

—Robert R. Morris
October 2004

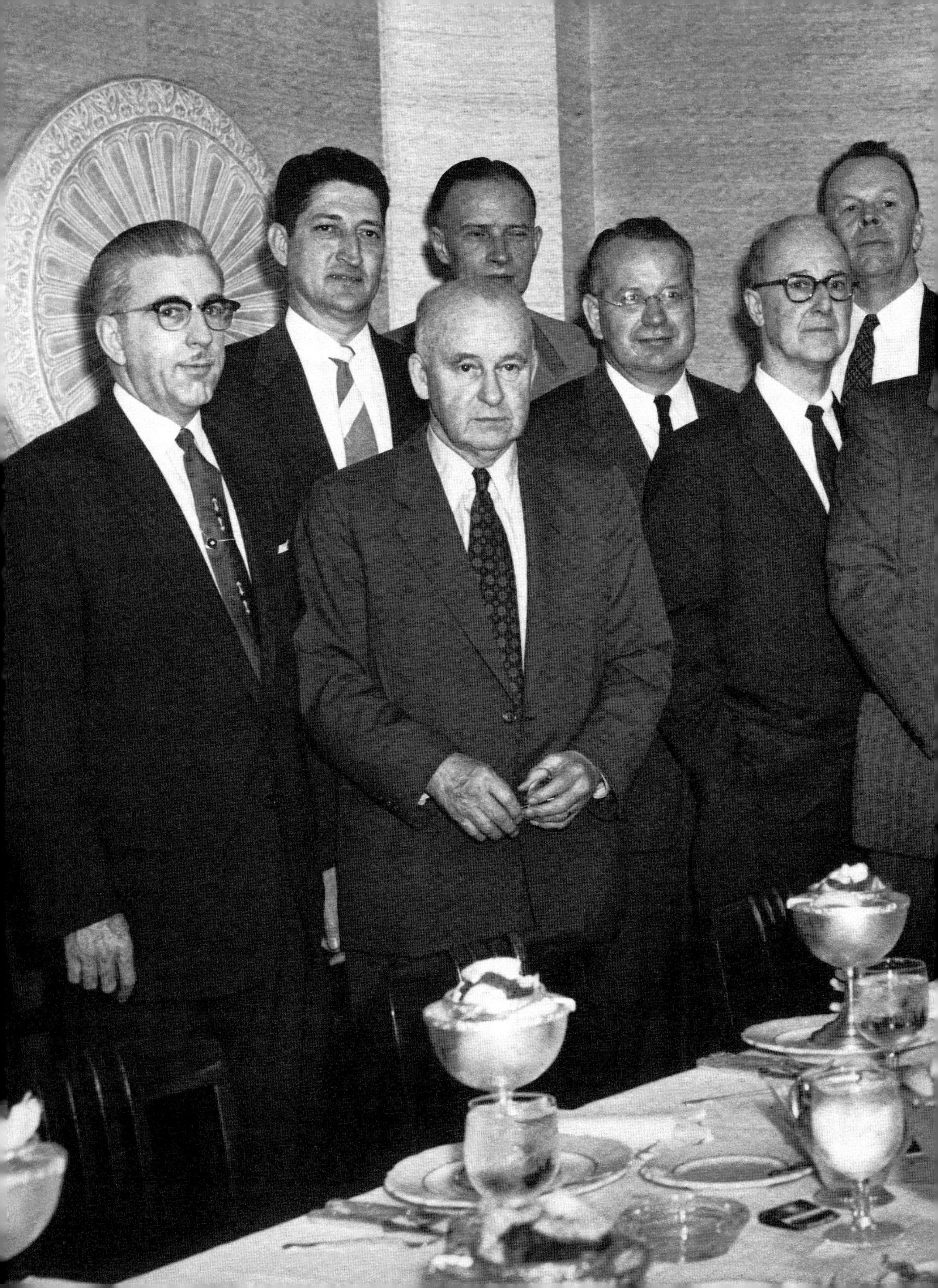

1

"To promote research and improve design of public food facilities..."

—Inaugural objective of the Food Facilities Engineering Society (ancestor of FCSI) at the meeting of the thirteen founders in Chicago on May 11, 1955

At the Beginning

The Foodservice Consultants Society International is the respected and truly professional organization of men and women offering design and management consulting services across the world. However, five decades ago, the profession existed, but only in the minds of those who believed in working together to promote their common good...

FCSI
FOODSERVICE CONSULTANTS SOCIETY INTERNATIONAL

"If I have a problem, or simply want to know something, all I need to do is pick up the phone and call," says FCSI European pioneer Bruno Brivio. "I have always received a good response!" Brivio adds.

Brivio, now retired from a career in foodservice consulting, lives near Zurich, Switzerland, more than 5,000 miles from the FCSI Louisville, Kentucky, headquarters. Yet Brivio enthusiastically promotes the organization that had its beginnings in Chicago and which for many years was focused almost exclusively on North America.

"The meetings and the seminars were places where I could discuss issues with the manufacturers and even our competitors—those benefits were matched only by the friendships I made," Brivio says.

Bruno Brivio's ebullient praise for and promotion of the Foodservice Consultants Society International is a recurring theme among the members, no matter where they live and work. His stance is held by hundreds of others—like-minded professionals who work in the foodservice industry as consultants.

His is not a profession at the top of international public awareness. Only a relative handful of the general public are even aware that foodservice consulting is an occupation. Yet for the men and women who toil each day offering their expertise and experience to institutional, business and industry, schools, and retail foodservice organizations, this is a profession that has grown in stature and influence in the decades since it was first recognized.

The benefits of FCSI to today's members could not have been dreamed even by the visionaries who founded the organization in the 1950s. But the founders made a leap of faith in doing so. Together, they created a profession, and a proud one at that.

A Pioneer

Fred Schmid had seen a lifetime full of changes in the American restaurant industry by the time World War II had ended. The world was very different and the changes that had taken place were only

Pictured on pages 16–17:
FCSI's oldest predecessor, the Food Facilities Engineering Society, was called into existence by the charter members on Wednesday, May 11, 1955. The foodservice consultants were organized by Fred Schmid and met during the National Restaurant Convention held in Chicago. This historic photo includes (from left): N. Bert Persson, W. B. "Pick" Holmes, J. Earle Stephens, John Forsyth, John Hargrave, Stacey Keates, Frank Hilliker, Sam Wells, Alvin Anderson, Ralph Mulhauser, Howard Post, Fred Schmid and Arthur Dana.

Bruno M. Brivio was one of the central figures in organizing the European Division of FCSI. However, in the organization's early days, much of the attention of the membership was focused on the United States and Canada.

the beginning. Schmid had started his own foodservice consulting firm in 1950, but his background had been heavily invested in the hotel and drugstore foodservice arena.

Born in Chicago in 1902, Schmid's early life was not unlike that of thousands of other immigrant Americans.[1] For many households, extensive education was an unaffordable luxury—and that was so in the Schmid family. After two years of high school, Fred Schmid had to join the workforce in order to help feed the family.

The teenager found a job as an office boy for Chicago's Albert Pick Hotel chain. Pick ran a large restaurant-equipment-producing subsidiary, headquartered on Chicago's South Side. Fred was assigned to the company's equipment engineering department and slowly learned all the aspects of restaurant and foodservice equipment.

"My father was an industrious, hardworking guy who soaked up knowledge of restaurant operations even though he had no formal training in the field," says Schmid's son Bob Schmid, himself a retired foodservice consultant.

"He was always driven by trying to better himself," the younger Schmid adds. Over his years with Albert Pick, Fred Schmid traveled the country, eventually designing kitchens and restaurants for Pick's new construction as well as redesigning facilities for the existing hotels Pick added to their holdings.

Along the way, Schmid acquired a fair understanding of restaurant architecture and allied design elements. Fred Schmid soon was named vice president at Albert Pick Hotels and acquired a stable of friends, acquaintances, and colleagues throughout the nation.

---

[1] The Schmid family had moved to Chicago after leaving their native Germany in the late 1800s.

In 1943, Schmid was hired away from Albert Pick by Justin Dart, Sr., who had just taken over direction of United Drug Companies, parent of Rexall Drug, a nationwide chain of drugstores, many of which had restaurants in them. Dart was on an expansion campaign and pinpointed the U.S. West Coast as the place for that expansion to take root. Dart tapped Schmid to be the company's vice president of construction and design for the firm, a job Schmid held until 1950. Schmid relocated to Rexall's new Los Angeles office.

Cultural Changes

Both Dart and Schmid clearly saw the changes coming over the foodservice horizon following World War II. Returning servicemen were marrying and starting families and new households in the millions. Yet there were very few apartments and homes for them to live in since there had been very little residential construction during the fifteen years preceding the end of the war.

During the Depression, few people in the United States had the money to build homes and during the war, rationing and restrictions on building materials prevented much new construction. By war's end, the demand for new homes was so bottled up that the housing market exploded into prominence.

Farmlands at the edges of the cities gave way to suburban developments. The new families needed furniture and appliances to put in them and one or two cars to put in the driveways since the workforce, ill-served by public transportation, needed individual transportation to get back and forth from work.

The new lifestyle afforded less time for sitting on the porch. As more time was spent commuting and more wives found the need to work, working couples began to eat out

Although FCSI was begun by many dedicated and involved individuals, Los Angeles–based restaurant and hotel consultant Fred Schmid is the organization's most respected "founding father."

FFES attracted new members easily and by the First Annual Meeting held in Chicago in May 1956, membership had almost doubled. At that meeting the inaugural Board of Governors took their places.

more often and the era gave rise to the emergence of the fast food restaurant chains.

The nationwide explosion in new construction combined with astonishing changes in the way average Americans lived and ate. The mom-and-pop diners serving up oval platters of hot pork sandwiches with mashed potatoes drenched in canned brown gravy and garnished with a parsley sprig gave way to fried chicken and hamburgers.

North Americans found their taste buds, became connoisseurs of fine wines, and ventured into exotic cuisines seldom tried by prior generations. The changes affected the very foundation of the restaurant industry and spawned a new profession—consultants well versed in foodservice to recommend design and equipment for the new waves of taste and demand spreading across the North American continent.

Fred Schmid saw what was happening. He also knew others who saw the future as well. In 1950, Fred left Rexall to start his own foodservice design consulting company, Fred Schmid Associates. At first, Schmid continued serving Rexall, now as an outside consultant. His consulting business quickly grew with an admirable list of clients.

Headquartered in Los Angeles, Fred Schmid quickly opened offices in Chicago and Honolulu. Despite his success, Fred knew there were only a handful of independent consultants like him and yearned for a means to strengthen the emerging profession and band together for continuing education and greater public awareness.

Gathering of Colleagues

"There weren't very many independent designers of foodservice in the country at that time," says Bob Schmid of those postwar years. "The reason is most professionals with those skills were working for equipment companies. Fred realized that things were getting more complicated and sophisticated," Bob Schmid adds.

Fred's vision was of a profession where independent foodservice consultants would be paid a fee for their services, much like architects.

"There were thirteen independent consultants besides my father who were basically doing the same things for the same amount of time and earning a good living," Bob Schmid says. "My father knew all of them."

As early as April 1952, Fred thought it was a good idea to gather with the other pioneers working in the fledgling field. He wrote to seven colleagues inviting them to join him for lunch at the 1952 National Restaurant Association Convention held in Chicago. In his invitation letters, Fred stressed, "…Since we're all in the profession of foodservice designing, nothing but mutual benefit could result from meeting informally and discussing any matters of general interest."[2]

We do not have records of their discussions at the 1952 meeting; however, the idea's time of forming a professional association had

---

[2] From *The First Twenty Years of the Food Facilities Consultants Society, 1955–1975*, published in 1975 by the Food Facilities Consultants Society, Samuel Crabtree, chairman, and Murl M. Schull, historian.

FCSI—CODE OF CONDUCT

Foundation

Foodservice Consultants Society International (FCSI) seeks to ensure that its Consultant (Professional, Senior Associate, and Associate) Members meet the highest levels of professional conduct and ethical standards related to the foodservice consultancy industry. In order to provide members with meaningful guidance, FCSI has developed the following Code of Conduct for its members to help ensure that they remain independent and objective.

This Code of Conduct is intended to increase the confidence and safety of all those engaging or relying on a member of FCSI.

The Code of Conduct shall be guided by three master principles:

- The Client's Interests
- The Public's Interests
- The Profession's Interests

Master Principle I—The Client's Interests

The interest of the client shall be paramount in all aspects of the specific work and general conduct of the member at all times.

Competence

A member shall only accept work that the member is fully qualified to perform. Members shall not make misleading statements about their ability or qualifications under any circumstances and shall refuse work, or refer it to other more qualified consultants, when they are not fully conversant with the subject matter, and would be jeopardizing the member's integrity and duty to perform the work to the highest standards.

Fee and Deliverable Arrangements

A member shall establish a scope, deliverable and fee arrangement with the client in writing, in advance of any substantive work being conducted on the client's behalf. Any additional work or any revision of work undertaken with the client shall be agreed to by the client in writing.

A member shall not receive income either directly from the supply of equipment, materials, facilities management services, or similar supply purchases by the client or indirectly through refunds or deductions from the supply of equipment, materials, facilities management services, or similar supply purchases by the client.

Conflict of Interest

A member shall avoid acting simultaneously for two or more clients in a potentially conflicting situation without informing all parties in advance and securing their agreement to the arrangement in writing.

A member shall inform a client of any interest which may reasonably be seen to impair the member's professional judgment.

A member shall disclose any known actual or potential conflicts of interest and provide full disclosure on any relationship which may have the potential to compromise the member's integrity or the quality of services rendered.

A member must disclose, in writing, any interest or arrangement with suppliers of any goods or services, other than consulting services, that may be requested by the client and the client must provide a countersignature signifying that the client understands the nature of the consultant/supplier relationship.

Client Employees

A member shall not take advantage of a client relationship by encouraging, unless by way of advertisement, an employee of a client to consider alternative employment without first discussing the opportunity with the client and obtaining the client's written permission to approach the employee.

Confidentiality

A member shall not disclose proprietary information obtained during the course of the assignment unless that information is already clearly in the public domain, or permission is obtained in writing, to disclose specific information for a specific purpose.

Independence and Objectivity

A member shall refrain from serving a client under any circumstance in which the member shall find herself/himself working in conditions which may impair the member's independence or judgment. A member should retain the ability to withdraw from an assignment in which the member loses her/his independence during the course of the engagement.

Client Understanding

The member shall ensure that the advice and recommendations the member presents are based upon his/her findings, analysis and experience in the industry, and are realistic, practical and presented to the client in a clear manner.

Disclosure

A member must declare and disclose to the client all relevant personal, financial, or other business interests, known to the member which may materially affect the client. The declaration must include but not be limited to:

- any directorship or controlling interest in any business in competition with the client
- any personal or financial relationship with the client, its employees, or a supplier
- any financial interest in goods or services recommended or supplied to the client either directly or by the consultant's employer
- any personal investment in the client organization or in its parent or subsidiary organizations
- any recent or current engagements in sensitive areas of work with a directly competitive firm of the client
- any current work or work completed in the past previous eighteen months for a third party on the opposite side of a transaction

Master Principle II—The Public's Interest

The interest of the public shall be highly considered and respected in all aspects of the specific work and general conduct of the member at all times.

Legal Responsibilities

A member shall act in accordance with applicable law of the jurisdiction in which the engagement is being conducted and within the member's own place of business at all times. The member shall not participate in any engagement which is in contravention of the law in the jurisdiction of the consultant, the client, or the physical engagement.

Representation

A member shall not represent the client or other members or any other interest without the express written permission of those the member represents, authorizing him/her to do so.

Public Decorum

The member must conduct herself/himself in a reasonable and respectful manner at all times in public, whether representing the membership or the profession.

Master Principle III—The Profession's Interest

The member shall be responsible to the interests of the foodservice consulting profession by endeavoring to enhance the standing and public image of the profession and the association within his/her community.

Knowledge

A member shall keep informed of the Code of Conduct at all times.

A member shall strive to keep abreast of developments in his/her specific areas of expertise.

A member shall comply with the Society's Continuing Professional Growth requirements.

Obligations to Other Members and the Profession at Large

A member shall respect the professional obligations of other members as set out in this Code of Conduct.

A member, when referring a third party, shall not make any commitments on behalf of the third party nor misrepresent the third party's qualifications.

A member shall not attempt to have another foodservice consultant's engagement terminated. Members shall not knowingly attempt to break an ongoing client relationship between another foodservice consultant and their client.

A member shall not approach another foodservice consultant's staff regarding alternative employment unless they have the other foodservice consultant's written agreement or follow normally acceptable recruitment procedures.

Publicity

A member, when promoting their work, firm, or herself/himself shall:

- Provide only factual and relevant information
- Neither be misleading nor unfair to others

Personal Conduct

A member shall operate her/his business and practice in such a manner to reflect normally accepted professional conduct.

A member shall maintain in good standing, her/his reputation and character at all times.

A member shall not give FCSI false, inaccurate, misleading, or incomplete information at any time.

A member shall not use or permit to be used the Society's name, initial, or seal inappropriately nor in any manner other than those set out in policy guidelines issued by the Board of Directors from time to time or with the express written permission of the FCSI Board of Directors.

apparently not yet come. Fred's vision for a Society percolated for a few more years. Relentless in his enthusiasm, Fred again called his colleagues together, this time at the 1955 National Restaurant Association Convention, held once again in Chicago in May of that year at the venerable Drake Hotel.

Twelve consultants met with Fred at the May 11, 1955 meeting[3] that had the following three tenets listed as common convictions:

1. *Those present saw the practice of foodservice equipment companies providing free planning services for prospective clients as a fallacy.*

2. *There was a clear need all over America for a more professional approach to the planning, designing, and engineering of all types of public feeding facilities.*

3. *That what few professional consultants there were at the time should band together to form some sort of Society for the interchange of ideas that would be of benefit to the entire industry.*[4]

Unlike the 1952 meeting which produced no consensus or action, this time those attending agreed upon a specific course of action. The thirteen consultants voted to form their own association to be called the Food Facilities Engineering Society (FFES).

The members drafted and approved a statement of organizational purpose: *To promote research and improve design of public food facilities.*

As his reward for coming up with the idea and encouraging the others to join together, Fred Schmid was elected president-

---

[3] One of Fred's colleagues, Hans J. Isler, a Detroit-based consultant, expressed enthusiastic interest in the meeting, but could not attend. Apparently ill at the time, Isler died the following September, however organization records list him as one of the fourteen charter members of what was to be called the Food Facilities Engineering Society.

[4] According to the authors of *The First Twenty Years of the Food Facilities Consultants Society, 1955–1975*, the three "convictions" were composed by Fred Schmid and either sent to those invited to attend the historic meeting or somehow distributed to them prior to their decision to form the Society.

treasurer of the organization. Ohio consultant John Hargrave was chosen vice president and Bert Persson of St. Paul, Minnesota, named secretary.[5] Three additional members were chosen to serve on the newly formed Executive Board of the organization.

The Charter Members drafted a list of "Eligibility Requirements" for FFES membership. These included:

—At least ten years experience in some phase of foodservice equipment planning, designing, etc.

—A minimum of one year as an established consultant in one's own business as a professional foodservice designer or consultant.

—No direct or indirect association with a foodservice equipment company or fabricator.

Now that the vision of Fred Schmid and the others had become a reality, the leaders had to settle down to contend with the "nitty-gritty" of forming the professional organization from scratch. There was no office, no staff, no files, no services. They all had to be developed from the ground up.

Murl M. Schull, one of Fred Schmid's business associates, served as the Society's first executive secretary. Schull received no salary and worked out of Schmid's Los Angeles office.

---

[5] The fourteen Charter Members of the Food Facilities Engineering Society were:
  Alvin W. Anderson (San Antonio, Texas)
  Arthur W. Dana (New York, New York)
  John R. Forsyth (Wild Rose, Wisconsin)
  John W. Hargrave (Montgomery, Ohio)
  Frank T. Hilliker (St. Louis, Missouri)
  W. B. "Pick" Holmes (Houston, Texas)
  Hans. J. Isler (Detroit, Michigan)
  Stacey Keates (Pittsburgh, Pennsylvania)
  Ralph J. Mulhauser (Houston, Texas)
  N. Bert Persson (St. Paul, Minnesota)
  Howard L. Post (New York, New York)
  Fred Schmid (Los Angeles, California)
  J. Earle Stephens (Detroit, Michigan)
  Sam V. Wells (Chicago, Illinois)

The FFES Second Annual Meeting took place at Chicago's Drake Hotel in May 1957.

Plans were made for a constitution and bylaws-writing committee and Fred was authorized to retain an attorney to form the non-profit corporation.

First Organizational Steps

At the start, the FFES was headquartered in Fred Schmid's office at 8032 West Third Street in Los Angeles. The Board retained Los Angeles attorney G. G. Baumen to incorporate the organization, which was done in California in June 1955.

The next six months were a whirlwind of organizing for the new professional Society. Fred depended heavily on several of his company's employees to assist in putting the components together for the Society's growth. Among them was Murl M. Schull,[6] who worked very hard to inaugurate a public awareness campaign of FFES' existence among allied professional organizations, trade groups, and trade publications.

---

[6] According to Bob Schmid, Schull was business manager in the Los Angeles office of Fred Schmid Associates.

The bylaws were completed and approved by the Charter Members in October 1955, and specified the following FFES membership classes:

—Independent consultant

—Consultant's technical or professional associates

—"Captive" consultant employed by a food operator or chain, or a government agency

—Specialist employed by an architect or engineer

— Educator

—Honorary member

Shortly after the bylaws were adopted, FFES accepted and approved an inaugural "Code of Ethics," written primarily by John W. Hargrave.

With the impressive progress of the first few months, Fred Schmid attended the Annual Meeting of the Food Service Equipment Industry, Inc. in November 1955 and updated their members of the advances taken by the young FFES.

The Start of Annual Meetings

The Charter Members agreed to hold the First Annual Meeting of the FFES in conjunction with the National Restaurant Association Convention in Chicago in May 1956. The one-day FFES meeting took place on May 9 and the members approved the acceptance of eleven new members, bringing the total membership to twenty-four.[7]

Fred Schmid invited representatives from related professional organizations, trade publication editors, and other industry representatives to attend some of the sessions and address the members. Through that, he set the stage for an FFES (and subsequently FCSI) tradition of continuous dialogue and information-sharing to benefit the members while also advancing the industry's awareness of FFES.

---

[7] One Charter Member, Hans Isler, had passed away in September 1955.

The charter member officers were re-elected by acclamation and continued serving through 1956–1957.[8] With the membership's enthusiastic support, Fred Schmid and his Executive Board planned for an expansion of the Annual Meeting program to two days when the Society met again in Chicago in May 1957.[9]

The 1957 program featured Society business exclusively on the first day, followed by presentations from and to the invited guests the following day. That year, FFES membership crept up a bit, now extended to twenty-six. In 1957, the members inaugurated the Board of Governors leadership model to assist the officers and provide a forum to identify and support emerging organizational leadership. Once again, the officers were re-elected to another one-year term.[10]

After two years of forming and building the Society, the work that had fallen on Fred Schmid had become formidable. In order to move the FFES to the next level of professionalism, the Board voted to establish the position of executive secretary. The day-to-day administrative duties of supervising the organization would be delegated to the executive secretary.

Fred Schmid's colleague, Murl M. Schull, was tapped to take over the role. Although he drew no salary from FFES,[11] Schull's travel and lodging expenses to attend and officiate at Annual Meetings were covered by FFES.

An Inaugural Milestone

In September 1957, the fledgling FFES achieved one of its first major accomplishments as a truly professional organization by joining

---

[8] John W. Hargrave, founding FFES vice president, died of injuries sustained in an auto accident in July 1956. J. Earl Stephens, another Charter Member, was chosen to replace him in a special mail ballot of members conducted in September 1956.

[9] The FFES once again met in conjunction with the National Restaurant Association Convention, held at the Drake Hotel in Chicago in May 1957.

[10] Fred Schmid, president-treasurer; J. Earl Stephens, vice president; N. Bert Persson, secretary.

[11] As one of Fred Schmid's employees, Schull's salary was covered through Schmid's company for the new part-time duties of FFES executive secretary.

3RD ANNUAL MEETING
FOOD FACILITIES ENGINEERING SOCIETY
Edgewater Beach Hotel — Chicago — May 3, 1958

At the 1958 Society meeting, Fred Schmid turned the gavel of the presidency over to Howard Post. The membership roster stood at thirty.

with Cornell University to inaugurate the school's Food Facilities Engineering Course Program. Members contributed financial support and literature, including drawings, specifications, depictions of completed projects, and photos of installations to provide documentation and archives for the program.

Cornell turned to FFES to recommend an appropriate and experienced member to teach the course.[12]

Transition

By the time FFES members gathered for their Third Annual Meeting in May 1958,[13] the formation and stabilization of the organization was complete. Fred Schmid, who had now completed three terms as FFES president, felt it was time to step aside and turn the honor and work over to others within the organization.

---

[12] FFES Vice President J. Earle Stephens was initially appointed as a full professor at Cornell to teach in and coordinate the program. Unfortunately, Stephens died suddenly in November 1957 and was succeeded by FFES Associate Member O. Ernest Bangs who had joined FFES that May.

[13] The 1958 FFES Annual Meeting was again held in conjunction with the National Restaurant Association Convention, held at Chicago's legendary pink art deco Edgewater Beach Hotel.

SOCIETY OBJECTIVES
Drafted by the Board of Directors in a 1995 Strategic Planning Session.

- Promote client usage of services provided by members
- Foster growth worldwide
- Establish and maintain communication with client-based associations
- Encourage the free exchange of ideas between members
- Maintain fiscal health of the Society
- Promote ethical industry practices
- Disseminate information useful or interesting to members
- Help members manage and promote their business
- Promote industry awareness of services provided by members
- Establish accreditation programs
- Ensure the future supply of qualified consultants
- Maintain a relationship with other industry groups
- Maintain a relationship with institutions of higher learning
- Promote social responsibility in the foodservice industry
- Recognize members' professional achievements

New Yorker Howard L. Post, one of the Charter Members, took over as president. The membership roster stood at thirty and the leadership team decided to "ramp up" the organization's visibility by commissioning a brochure with a membership listing, the Code of Ethics, a description of services FFES members rendered, and a schedule of fees for those services.

In addition, members manned the first-ever FFES display booth at the National Restaurant Association Convention, further highlighting the young Society's viability and vibrancy.

That year, however, FFES archives report the first mention of a possible naming controversy, a controversy that would recur and grow over the next few years, eventually resulting in the need to rename the organization. Several FFES members reported to the leadership that in their home states, they were having issues with state registration boards over their use of the word engineer on their letterheads. Although the occasional issue over the word concerned some FFES members, no action was taken at that time. Conditions, however, would eventually force a change.

ISFSC

Another matter of concern and interest to FFES members was the formation of what was apparently a competing professional organization: the International Society of Food Service Consultants (ISFSC).[14]

The continuing ideological struggle over independent consultants vs. those employed by equipment manufacturers resulted in

[14] Bob Schmid relates that ISFSC began in the late 1950s, after a few manufacturers' equipment dealers were turned down for FFES membership because of their relationship to the sale of equipment. Schmid says that the men started their own organization as a protest. ISFSC, however, also found a niche and grew in the ensuing years as well.

The International Society of Food Service Consultants began in 1958 as a competing organization to FFES. At the charter meeting held in Chicago on May 4, were (starting at the head of the table closest to the camera and continued clockwise) Reg Venn, Vincent Antonelli, Joseph Berger, James Brown, Ahmet Dervishi, John Cini, Robert Hickman, Burt Higgins, John Fellers, Eldon Miller, George Zipfel, Harry Friedman, Saul Blickman, Norman Brady, Milton Shier, Ben Freed, LaMont Van Dell, Donald Lundberg, Harry Todd, Maurice Lafiteau, Syd Sobel, Bert Marshall, M. Robbins, and Lester Florreich.

When the FFES gathered for their Fourth Annual Meeting in Chicago in 1959, Leopoldine Wiard joined the men as the first female member of the Society.

several of the latter being excluded from FFES membership. Understandably, the rejected applicants felt they had a great deal they could add through association with others in similar lines. They did not share the "purist" view that only "pure" independent consultants should be members of FFES. Several decided to form their own professional organization.

"In October 1957, Burton Higgins, the head of a Detroit foodservice consulting firm, asked me to meet with him and several other men, including George Zipfel and Harry Friedman," says John Fellers, one of the early members of ISFSC. Higgins proposed the idea of a society. "We drew up a list of names and started asking others to join us," Fellers adds. "We also asked them for $15.00 in dues!"

By the time of the May 1958 National Restaurant Show, they were ready to charter their organization. The now twenty-four men gathered at Chicago's Knickerbocker Hotel[15] on May 4 and formed the International Society of Food Service Consultants (ISFSC).

---

[15] The Charter meeting of ISFSC was held in the downtown Chicago hotel while the members were in the city attending the National Restaurant Association Convention. Simultaneously, FFES held its Third Annual Meeting.

Harry Friedman served as the group's first president. Fellers served as the Secretary, a job he would hold on a part-time basis for the next five years. In its early years and through the 1960s, ISFSC was the larger and healthier of the two competing organizations and grew at a slightly faster rate than FFES.

A Broad Scope

From the start, ISFSC was more innovative than FFES. ISFSC was also the first to look beyond the North American continent. Fellers credits ISFSC Founding President Harry Friedman as being the initial proponent of a global outlook for the organization.

"From the start, Harry Friedman urged us to go international," Fellers recalls. "He told us to seek out and get to know the great foodservice designers in Europe and South America," Fellers says. Friedman had extensive contacts in Europe since his firm had been working with Movenpick, a Swiss restaurant/cafeteria chain.

The innovative strain in ISFSC was also enhanced by the group's second president, the flamboyant Richard Flambert.

"When Richard Flambert came in, he took over the room; he was a pint-sized de Gaulle!"[16] Fellers adds about the bigger-than-life Flambert. But Flambert[17] put his mark on the young organization and steered it towards many new concepts. He stressed the importance of the annual programs and seminars and soon ISFSC became well-known for the outstanding, informative, and beneficial programs put on for its members.

---

[16] Charles de Gaulle was a French general who led the resistance movement during the German occupation in World War II and also served as French president on two occasions, the latter ending in 1969. De Gaulle had a reputation for egotism and intransigence and was considered "difficult" by even his closest advisers.

[17] John Fellers relates that there may have been an element of personal competition at the start of ISFSC, since Flambert and FFES founder Fred Schmid were fierce competitors in foodservice consulting. Both Schmid and Flambert operated nationwide consulting firms from their California headquarters.

—Background material for this section was obtained from: *The First Twenty Years of the Food Facilities Consultants Society, 1955–1975*, published in 1975 by the Food Facilities Consultants Society, Samuel Crabtree, chairman, and Murl M. Schull, historian.

ISFSC also began what would become FCSI's prestigious professional publication, *The Consultant*, in 1968.[18]

During the 1960s, ISFSC continued to stress international focus and excellent programs. When Earl Triplett concluded his term as ISFSC president in 1965, he turned to serving as the organization's executive secretary, running the group for many years afterwards.

In an era of male-domination of many fields, neither the FFES nor the ISFSC were unique in their male-only membership for the first few years. However, FFES did make a bold move in 1959, when Leopoldine H. Wiard was accepted as the first female member.[19]

As the members of the FFES and ISFSC were poised to enter the 1960s, they could look back with pride on the slow but steady birth, growth, and acceptance of their organizations. However, they could not have imagined how the Society would look by the end of one of the most tumultuous decades of the twentieth century. ■

---

[18] ISFSC's professional journal, *The Consultant*, was edited for many years by Asa K. Gaylord, who retired in 1976. That year, Gaylord turned the editing and publishing duties of the publication over to C. Russell Nickel, who served a term as ISFSC president.

[19] Although FFES was breaking ground by encouraging women to join the Society at that time, for the next decade, the roster only boasts one or two women at a time. That situation would rapidly change in the 1970s.

The 1979 Seminar and
Annual Meeting Report

the Consultant

Volume XIII, No.1 July 1979

**Foodservice Consultants
Society International**

FOOD FACILITIES ENGINEERING SOCIETY
FIFTH ANNUAL MEETING
Sheraton-Blackstone Hotel — Chicago — May 7-8, 1960

"Our organization provides a meeting place for consultants to share experiences and knowledge..."

—John Cini, FCSI Fellow, ISFSC former president, and a member since 1958

Chicago
60-1513

Slow Yet Steady

With FFES established, the constant attention of the Board now turned to increasing membership and awareness of their role in the industry. Both initiatives would be tested by controversy and competition during the 1960s and 1970s...

When Frank Hilliker became FFES president in 1960, there were forty-nine members. The Annual Meetings, held traditionally in conjunction with the National Restaurant Association Convention, were well-attended and greatly anticipated by FFES members. That year, the leadership felt it necessary to expand the FFES future Annual Meeting Program to three days from two.

When the FFES met for their Sixth Annual Meeting in May 1961, the issue of the word *Engineering* in the Society's name was again brought up for prominent discussion. Registration officials in the state of New Jersey, in particular, had informed FFES members there that they could not continue to use the term *engineer* to describe the services they performed for their clients.

FFES members in that state and others where the controversy had once again appeared decided to call themselves "foodservice consultants" or "food facilities consultants" instead of "engineers." The Board recommended that all members consider using these descriptive terms. However, the name of the organization, Food Facilities Engineering Society was not to be changed at this time, despite the ever-looming difficulties with state registration boards as well as professionals who worked in traditional engineering endeavors. This issue simply would not go away and would eventually return.

Changes

At the 1962 FFES Annual Meeting, Arthur W. Dana became the organization's fourth president, elected by the organization's sixty-eight members. To better serve the geographically diverse members, some of whom were Canadians, the Society made two moves which were expanded greatly in future years.

First, the Canadian members were to become the first regional chapter of the organization and began calling themselves members of the "Canadian Chapter of the FFES." Second, a regional meeting

Pictured on pages 44–45:
FFES had grown to forty-nine members by the time of the Society's Fifth Annual Meeting held in Chicago in May 1960.

Opposite:
When the FFES met for their Sixth Annual Meeting in Chicago in 1961, there were already serious demands from several engineering sectors demanding the Society remove the word *Engineering* from the organization's official name.

SOCIETY PUBLICATIONS

The Consultant is FCSI's first-rate quarterly magazine featuring the latest member and Society news, profiles of member projects, and reports on new trends and techniques. Each must-read issue contains many articles submitted by members and other recognized professionals in the foodservice industry.

The Forum is a monthly newsletter distributed by e-mail which contains news for and about the Society and the foodservice industry at large.

Membership Directory
The FCSI *Membership Directory*, published annually, is an easy reference of fellow Society members and provides information that can be used to identify consultants for potential partnering opportunities. The directory is also available to foodservice operators upon request.

separate from the annual gathering at the National Restaurant Association Convention took place in New York City.[20]

The Society's administrative duties now had also grown to the point that the Board authorized the hiring of a part-time executive secretary to take over the day-to-day functions.[21] In December 1962, the Board hired Arthur B. Olian as the FFES' first professional executive secretary.

Olian, a trained attorney who ran his own advertising and public relations firm in Pennsylvania, had considerable experience in foodservice-related endeavors. Since 1950, he had provided similar duties for Marketing Agents for the Food Service Industry[22] (MAFSI), serving as that organization's part-time executive secretary.

---

[20] Called the first "Eastern Regional Meeting." In 1966, the now-successful New York/Eastern convocation was renamed the Fall Meeting.

[21] Up until this point, administrative duties had been handled by Murl M. Schull, at little cost to the FFES, as Schull worked out of Fred Schmid's consulting firm headquarters in Los Angeles. As thanks for his years of work, FFES named Schull a Lifetime Honorary Member for his hard work and dedication to the organization.

[22] Renamed the "Manufacturers' Agents Association for the Foodservice Industry" in the 1990s.

In January 1963, all FFES files and funds were transferred from Schmid's Los Angeles office to Olian's office in Harrisburg, Pennsylvania. Olian promptly began writing and editing the first FFES regular publication, *F.F.E.S. News*, in February 1963. The FFES Board voted to increase dues in order to cover the expenses and salary of the executive secretary.

Movement to Solve Issues

In 1964, John Philips took over the role of FFES president and found he had two pressing issues to contend with. That year, a Texas FFES member was sued by an architect for using the term *engineering* in his letterhead and correspondence. A Pennsylvania FFES member was repeatedly questioned by the local society of engineers for using the FFES stamp/seal, which, of course, contained the word *engineering*. Other members reported increasing instances of similar inquiries. The Society stuck to their original name, but now cautioned members in the areas where the continuing instances took place to discontinue using the offending word as well as the FFES official stamp. The move bought a little more time.

There was also a growing professional divide between those who were independent consultants and those who provided facilities consulting and design services, but were employed by equipment dealers. Each group knew they shared much in common with the others, however, FFES explicitly refused membership to those associated with the sale of equipment. The dealer designers had formed their own, competing organization, ISFSC, to meet their own professional growth needs.

Having two organizations competing in the same arena for the same very small pool of professional foodservice consultants seemed wasteful and destructive to many members of each group. However, there were many in FFES who were adamant about the separation of independent consultants and dealers providing design services. The issue was a conundrum not easily solved.

During the early 1960s, the ISFSC was the first of the two competing organizations to embrace members from "overseas." Here, ISFSC Board members confer. From left: Unidentified, George Zipfel, John W. Stokes, Richard Flambert, Unidentified, Asa Gaylord, John Fellers, Harry Friedman, Unidentified, Syd Sobel, and Charlotte May Link.

However, in order to allow for information sharing and collegiality, in 1965, both groups met jointly for a liaison session at the May National Restaurant Association Convention held at Chicago's sprawling McCormick Place Convention Center.

In the mid-1960s, FFES membership eligibility was broadened to include, for the first time, so-called "captive" consultants—employees of architectural firms or other foodservice-related companies. With the influx of new members, the total FFES roster surpassed one hundred for the first time.

With these new members, the unending situation over the use of the word *engineering* reached a critical mass, so after a great deal of soul-searching, discussion, and the threat of litigation from many quarters, the FFES membership acquiesced to what seemed to be a no-win battle. In May 1968, at the Thirteenth Annual Meeting, the organization's name was changed from the Food Facilities Engineering Society (FFES) to the Food Facilities Consultants

Society (FFCS). The nonprofit corporation was now registered in Pennsylvania, where Executive Secretary Arthur Olian maintained FFCS files, accounts, and the headquarters' office.

Internal Stability; External Tumult

With membership now at 108, Carl Hansen took the reins as president of the FFCS in 1968. The most pressing and cantankerous issues facing the FFCS had been dealt with. The only remaining concern was the continuing existence of two organizations competing for the relatively paltry number of foodservice professionals—FFCS and ISFSC. The two organizations sported about the same number of members, and although there was a great amount of common ground covered by each, there was still the thorny issue of independent consultants versus dealers.

Some members of both organizations felt the two groups could successfully merge and thereby serve all of the members better through the obvious strength in numbers and economies of scale in operational overhead for a new, single professional organization. This group was in the minority, although they continued to press for a union of the two groups, which shared such similar professional paths.

John Fellers (left) presents Wid Neibert with a plaque of appreciation at an ISFSC meeting. Both Fellers and Neibert served as ISFSC presidents.

Internally, both FFCS and ISFSC were stable, serving their members in an industry that was growing. For most, the hospitality and restaurant industries represented solid, reliable, traditional American values. Restaurants, chains, institutions, and hotels served business travelers and families for the most part.

Both organizations, and the foodservice industry they served, continued to grow and work with organizations placing new restaurant facilities or redesigning existing operations to reflect new behavior patterns and eating habits of the people.

Faster, more dependable service with reliably good quality food in a comfortable, clean setting with easy parking availability became the mantra of the foodservice industry at the same time protestors took to the streets to challenge the status quo.

Like the society at large, which brought about significant social change during the 1970s, the new decade also brought to FFCS and ISFSC considerable changes as well.

Into the 1970s

Keith Little was elected president of FFCS in May 1970 at the Fifteenth Annual Meeting of the FFCS at the Chicago Water

Richard Flambert (left) is congratulated by ISFSC President Wid O. Neibert. The legendary Flambert served ISFSC in a manner similar to that of Fred Schmid at FFES.

At the FFES Seventh Annual Meeting in Chicago in 1962, the members decided to add a fall meeting in New York to the schedule.

Tower Inn. There were 128 members now and the pace of new membership applications was beginning to pick up again.

That year, FFCS formalized the Canadian Chapter, which had been operating informally as a chapter in name only for several years. Now, Canadian Jacques Beauchemin took the role of guiding the Canadian Chapter, and with that, the organization took its first tentative steps towards internationalization—a theme that would become very important to the Society two decades later.

In 1971, the officers, headed by Keith Little, were elected for another term at the Annual Meeting. By this time, a significant number of the Charter Members of then-FFES had moved into retirement. In a nod to their visionary role, FFCS established a new membership category, Member Emeritus, designed specifically to provide continuing association with the Society for those members who retired from active practice.[23]

That year, at the Sixteenth Annual FFCS Meeting in May, the members brought up—again—the concept of a merger with ISFSC. In a vote taken on the issue, FFCS members overwhelmingly rejected the initiative. However, the members did feel that it would be a good and productive idea to schedule a joint session and reception with ISFSC at the 1972 Annual Meeting at the National Restaurant Association Convention.

A Tragedy and Aftermath

In November 1971, FFCS Executive Secretary Arthur Olian died suddenly of a heart attack. Olian had been serving in the role since January 1963 and FFCS members were happy with his performance and shocked by the unexpected turn of events.[24]

Immediately, the Board began a search for Olian's replacement.[25] The search took until May 1972, when the Board hired Ellis Murphy as the new FFCS executive secretary.[26]

Samuel Crabtree worked with many others to smooth the way for a merger between FFES and ISFSC.

[23] Up until this time, those members who retired also resigned from FFCS, which was unfortunate, since so many members of the small organization had made close friends among the other members. They valued the social interaction as well as the professional support and collegiality, and with the Emeritus Membership classification, could continue to attend meetings and keep abreast of professional developments while at the same time maintain their social circle of lifetime friends.

[24] Olian's sudden death was also a deep tragedy for the members of MAFSI, (the marketing agents for the Foodservice Industry). Olian had been executive secretary for that professional organization for more than twenty years, originally taking the job in 1950.

[25] According to Murl M. Schull, the officers of both FFCS and MAFSI spent considerable time and personal expense traveling and interviewing candidates to succeed Olian. Apparently, there was no provision in the FFCS budget to cover job search expenses for the position of executive secretary.

[26] Wisely, MAFSI decided to choose someone else as their executive secretary, rather than face the possibility of a joint loss again at some point in the future.

The long gap between executive secretaries and the unique way Olian kept organizational records[27] proved to be a hardship for the organization and its members. Eventually, FFCS records and files were moved from Olian's Harrisburg, Pennsylvania offices to Murphy's headquarters in Chicago. Part of Murphy's assignment was to develop a new look for the organization's regular newsletter. Later that year, Murphy produced *FFCS Spec Sheet* which featured a more current layout and photos. *FFCS Spec Sheet* replaced the *F.F.E.S. News* which had been started by Arthur Olian in 1963.

In 1972, Samuel Crabtree was elected FFCS president and was immediately consumed by yet another executive secretary crisis. Ellis Murphy, hired for the role the prior May, resigned.

"The first job I had was to find a new executive secretary," says Sam Crabtree of his first days as FFCS president. After another considerable period of searching for the right candidate to tap for the important role, Crabtree and the Board settled upon a solution that appeared tailor-made for the FFCS. Longtime FFCS member (since 1956) Henry H. Rothman, who had progressed to membership on the Board of Governors, expressed a desire to take the job. Receiving a positive reaction from other members of FFCS leadership, Rothman resigned from the Board and retired from active consulting practice to take the position.

Appointed the third executive secretary at the Eighteenth Annual Meeting in May 1973, Rothman used the next several months as a

Henry H. Rothman served the Society in several capacities, starting as a member in 1956, moving to the Board of Governors, and eventually resigning as a consultant to take over as Society executive secretary in 1973.

---

[27] According to information in *The First Twenty Years of the Food Facilities Consultants Society*, Arthur Olian apparently functioned as a "one man band," seldom sharing information about his files or work for FFCS with his associates. As a result, it was very difficult to figure out Olian's arcane record-keeping system. There was a protracted period of repeated errors in billings and dues crediting. The difficult situation may have contributed to the short tenure of Olian's successor, Ellis Murphy, who stayed in the position less than a year.

period of transition, assuming the full responsibilities of the job in August. Files and records were once again trucked cross-country, from Murphy's Chicago offices to Rothman's Sea Cliff, New York headquarters.

Rothman's experience in foodservice consulting would provide a great boost to the organization's daily operations, as Rothman had a clear understanding of the profession. Even after almost twenty years in existence, the overall pool of people calling themselves foodservice consultants in the 1970s was still very small, making the field a highly niche-oriented one. The Board, together with members, welcomed Rothman's appointment, since the FFCS would now be administered by someone who actually had extensive experience working in the field.[28]

More Merger Moves

Henry Rothman's approach to his job as executive secretary had a very beneficial effect upon FFCS members and the organization. Rhoda and Henry Rothman teamed up to produce interesting and

Starting in the 1960s, the leadership of FFES and ISFSC held a series of joint meetings, each exploring the possibility of working more closely together. As always, the issue of independent consultants versus those working for manufacturers presented a significant impediment which was not resolved until the late 1970s.

---

[28] Henry Rothman's wife, Rhoda, was also quite knowledgeable about the foodservice consulting field and assisted her husband in providing member services. The two worked as a team and were often seen together at FFCS events for many years.

Members of Food Facilities Consulting Society (FFCS) in 1977.

efficiently run programs, as well as organizing special events for the Board of Governors and the general membership.

Part of the approach included a continuing dialogue with the leadership and members of the ISFSC. Although FFCS membership stood at 127 in 1974, marking a significant increase from the original fourteen who founded the group in 1955, few could say that the organization had grown dramatically in the ensuing twenty years. FFCS was still a small group, as was ISFSC.[29]

The pace and number of joint events slowly grew. In September 1973, Rothman organized a joint FFCS/ISFSC dinner and seminar at the NAFEM[30] Meeting in Dallas. The topic of the seminar also predicted the future internationalization of the organizations, as speakers addressed the issue of "Using Your Skill Overseas."

---

[29] ISFSC veteran John Fellers says that although there was considerable animosity between many members of ISFSC and FFES/FFCS at their starts, by the 1970s, many of the founders of each group had stepped back from leadership or retired. The younger members who had joined since the early days had no recollection of the prior ill will. Since there was really not enough room in the profession for two competing organizations, many of the members easily moved towards supporting a merger of the two. The issue of "independence" however, would continue to fester until eventually common ground would be found between the two organizations.

[30] The National Association of Food Equipment Manufacturers.

AWARDS

Awards for Excellence in Design and Management Advisory Services (MAS)

Each year the Society presents awards to consultant members in recognition of outstanding consulting projects. These awards are judged by a recognized panel of member peers.

Manufacturer of the Year

This award, formerly known as the Award for Distinguished Development, recognizes Allied Members of FCSI who have demonstrated exceptional innovation in research and development. The award salutes the company for best satisfying the foodservice industry's needs and contributing to the overall effectiveness in the areas of safety, operation, and/or efficiency in customer service.

FCSI Service Award

This award is presented to an individual who has demonstrated throughout the year extraordinary efforts in contributing to the betterment of the Society through dedication, commitment, loyalty, creativity, and enthusiastic service.

The Trendsetter Award

This award is presented to an individual who best exemplifies innovation, creativity and unique and lasting contributions to the foodservice industry.

The Consultant Article Awards

All contributions to *The Consultant* deserve recognition, but each year two authors are selected for special honors. Awards are presented at the Annual Conference for the best articles published in the preceding year by a consultant member and by an allied member.

As part of the Nineteenth Annual Meeting of the FFCS in Chicago in May 1974, a joint seminar and luncheon with ISFSC was part of the program.

Slowly, despite continuing philosophical resistance, the membership of each organization was coming to the realization that merging the two into one would make more sense from a representational and efficiency point of view.

The following year, joint sessions of the two groups again took place at the FFCS Twentieth Annual Meeting. One of the highlights presented to the members in 1975 was the publication of the first-ever "Glossary of Foodservice Equipment." Under development by FFCS members for quite some time, the "Glossary" started life as a simple listing of foodservice equipment for the use of members in contract drawings. However, under the Board's guidance, the "Glossary" evolved into a document of standardization for all members. The "Glossary," published by *Food Service Equipment Dealer Magazine*, was carried in the journal's December 1975 issue and became a much-sought-after resource for consulting professionals, educators, and students in the hospitality industry.

The "Glossary of Food Service Equipment" represented a milestone accomplishment advancing the objectives and professionalism of FFCS members.

The Milestone Merger

Through 1975 and 1976, the FFCS members and officers were concentrating on improving programs that addressed the real-world conditions in which foodservice consultants found themselves.

The concerns were echoed in FFCS program presentations, which advised members on dealing with rapidly increasing construction and equipment costs. The poor economic conditions were exacerbated by the oil crisis, resulting in a slowdown in demand for the services of FFCS members. The pace of new construction of restaurants, hotels, and institutions slowed. With it the demand for FFCS services stagnated.

By this time, the members saw that now, more than ever before, joining forces would work to the benefit of everyone working in the foodservice consulting profession.

From left: Bob Schmid, Bill Merz, and Fred Schmid participate in the historic merger vote in 1978.

By the time the Society held its Annual Meeting in 1970, the members agreed to drop the word *Engineering* from their name, replacing it with *Consultants*.

James H. Little was elected FFCS president in May 1977. The son of prior FFCS President Keith Little,[31] Jim seized upon the timing and opportunity to bring the two groups together. He rallied the Board to support what would result in a two-year Unification Study Committee with representatives of both FFCS and ISFSC. Jim Little assigned his vice president, William Eaton, to the role of chairing the Unification Study Committee.

"When I was president, we went through all of the negotiations and set the stage for the merger," Little says of the momentous time in FFCS history. "The major issue was that the members of the FFCS were all purely consultants, working with consulting firms, whereas many members of the ISFSC worked for a dealer or an architect. There was strong feeling among a number of people that we had to remain pure," Little adds with understatement.

Slowly, working together with another prime mover supporting the merger, Frank Giampietro,[32] a compromise position emerged,

---

[31] Keith Little joined FFES in 1959 and served two terms as president, from 1970 to 1972. According to his son James Little, Keith was the first Canadian member of the organization and the first Canadian to serve as the Society's president.

[32] Frank N. Giampietro was a member of both ISFSC and FFCS and served as FFCS president in 1976–1977.

which helped to settle the concerns of many, but not all, members. Giampietro felt passionately that the two groups could and should find a means to accommodate their intense ideological differences.

"The major contention was dealing with those who derived income from the sale of equipment," Eaton says. The long-held thought among FFCS members was that one could not be independent in judgment if you gained by the sale of equipment. However, others pointed out that not all ISFSC members were manufacturer representatives or recipients of commissions on sales.

The solution was to "grandfather" in all ISFSC members at the time of a possible merger. "We then established an exclusion which still exists today," Eaton says. "Anyone who manufactures, markets, sells, or distributes foodservice equipment would be excluded going forward."

The discussion and their outcomes were not without contention. "There were some heated moments," Eaton adds.

Right:
James H. Little was the first FFES/FFCS president whose father also served in the role. James Little worked with a Unification Committee to bring about the historic merger in 1979, thus holding the distinction as the last FFCS president.

Left:
In 1979, William Eaton became the first president of the now-merged Foodservice Consultants Society International.

—Background material for this section was obtained from: www.mafsi.org, the website for the Manufacturers' Agents Association for the Foodservice Industry (MAFSI), Atlanta, GA © 2004 MAFSI, and; *The First Twenty Years of the Food Facilities Consultants Society, 1955–1975*, published in 1975 by the Food Facilities Consultants Society, Samuel Crabtree, chairman, and Murl M. Schull, historian.

Left:
Frank Giampietro had been a member of both FFCS and ISFSC and was a central figure in forging a workable agreement uniting the two organizations.

Right:
Russ Nickel (left) presents Joe Laschober with an engraved silver tray to commemorate his term as ISFSC president.

"It was hotly contested and argued!" says former FFCS President Sam Crabtree, an active participant in the merger discussions. Crabtree says that several FFCS and ISFSC members resigned over the issue and never returned to the organization.

"I had been on the verge of resigning several times myself," Crabtree adds. "But I felt it was better to be looking from the inside out than from the outside in." Crabtree mourned the loss of the members. "They never came back and I was awfully sorry to lose them. I understood their position and even agreed with them. But sometimes you have to bend a little bit," Crabtree says philosophically.

After two years of very difficult and intense work, the Unification Study Committee prepared a presentation of their final recommendation. The informational session was scheduled for the joint meeting of the two organizations at the May 1978 National Restaurant Association Convention in Chicago.[33]

---

[33] The 1978 NRA convention would mark the Twenty-third Annual FFCS meeting and the twentieth for the ISFSC.

Attendees at the 1977 Annual Conference and joint meeting.

After twenty years of independent existence, the memberships of both the FFCS and ISFSC were slated to vote for or against the proposed merger of the two organizations. The atmosphere of the voting event, which was held on Saturday morning, May 20, 1978, was charged with anticipation.

The outcome of the balloting would profoundly change the course of the future for both the FFCS and the ISFSC. ■

The historic gathering of the members of the ISFSC and the FFCS in 1978.

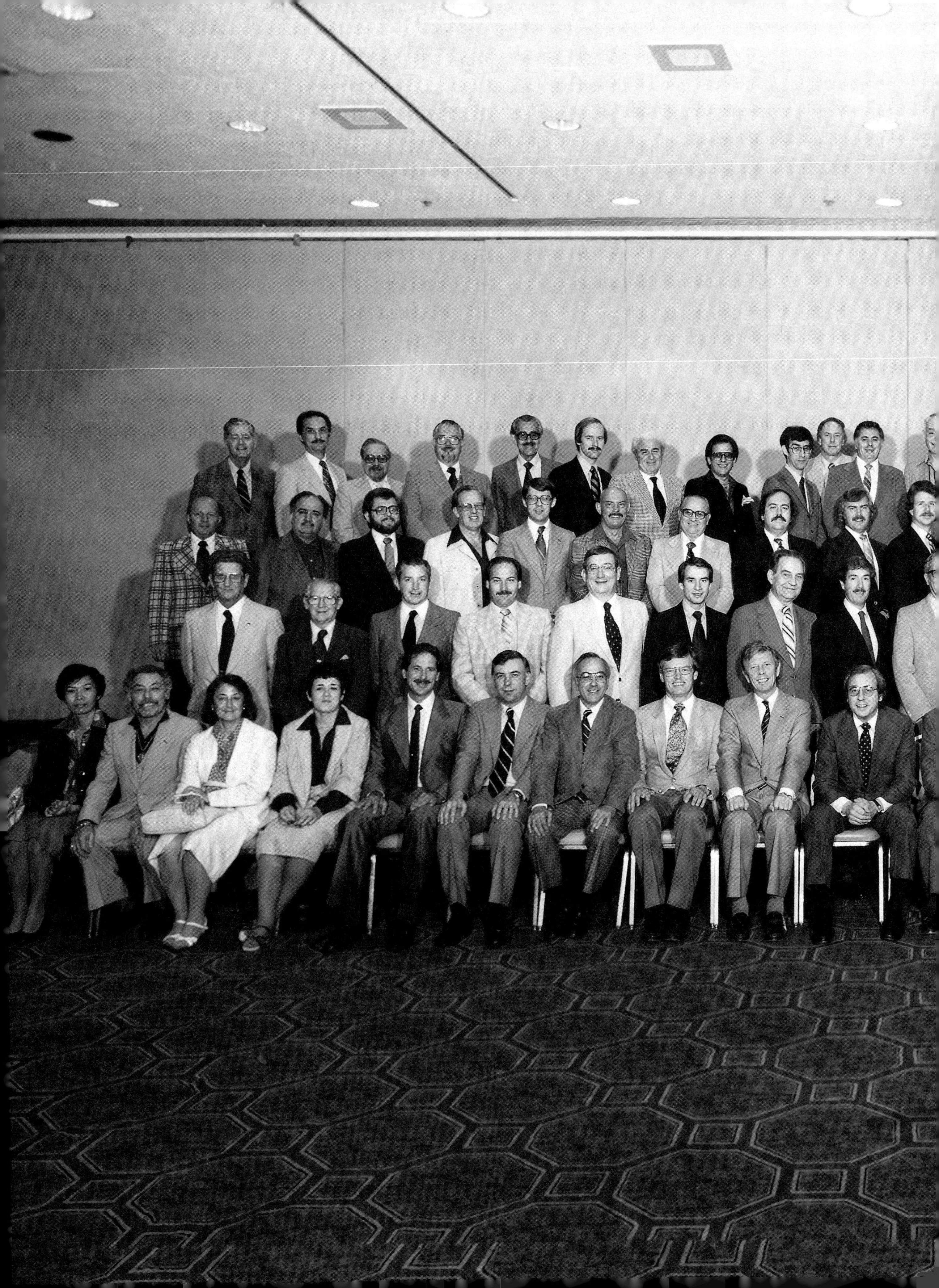

3

"We spent much of that first year making sure the best elements that had been in ISFSC and FFCS were brought into the new organization..."

—William V. Eaton, First president of the combined Foodservice Consultants Society International

A Unified Front

The historic vote taken on May 20, 1978, resulted in strong support for the merger of the two competing organizations. Over the course of the next year, teams of committee members worked over the minutiae of logistics in making one entity out of two. The time was not without considerable stress...

"We spent the first couple of years just getting to know each other," says Robert H. Kaiser, ISFSC president at the time the members approved the merger of the two organizations. "We had discussions on how we could control dealer-members, which made everyone happier," Kaiser adds.

The contentious issues had been resolved with the merger, so the leadership of each organization now devoted their time to preparing for the actual functioning merger to take place on May 1, 1979. The groups had to develop a new set of bylaws and operations to govern the new entity.

The new name for the unified organization was the Foodservice Consultants Society International. The joint Board determined that the Society needed professional management and moved to hire a firm which placed a new executive director into the position held since 1973 by Henry Rothman. The headquarters office was now moved from Rothman's Sea Cliff, New York facility to the management company's offices in Glenview, Illinois.

A New Day and a Stumble

The First Annual Meeting of the Foodservice Consultants Society International took place in Chicago in May 1979. Bill Eaton was elected as FCSI's first president and inaugurated a period of great hope and expectations.

What happened, in reality, was a protracted period of fiscal disaster, which if left unchecked, could very well have doomed the new organization to a premature and embarrassing demise.

The FCSI Board had good intentions by deciding to turn the day-to-day management of the organization over to experienced association management professionals. The former FFCS had left the management capabilities of Henry Rothman.

"It was the wrong decision," Bill Eaton says of the move at the start of FCSI. "The management company really didn't understand our organization, nor did they understand how to manage us and put

Pictured on pages 44–45:
In 1980, the new Foodservice Consultants Society International Annual Seminar was held for the first time in Miami.

Opposite:
The FCSI Board of Directors in 1980. Back row from left: Murray Perl, Bill Eaton, Dennis Glore, Stig Westberg, Tom Pappas, and Bob Whitney. Front row: Tony Clevenger, Paul Hysen, Charlie Wood, and Ron Kooser.

In 1980, C. Russell Nickel became executive director of the FCSI. Nickel had at one time been president of ISFSC.

in the necessary programs that would bring income and keep us solvent," Eaton adds.

During the first year of existence, FCSI went through two executive directors appointed by the management company and the Society soon experienced dire financial circumstances. "We were spending a lot of money making our name known, but it was money we did not have," Eaton says of the extensive public relations campaign allied to the startup of the new combined Society.

Dues were quite low and income from seminars and special events covered their costs but did not enhance the Society's treasury.

After the troubling first year, the FCSI Board took drastic actions, severing the agreement with the Illinois management company. "We went hat in hand and invited Russ Nickel to help bail us out," Eaton says.

In May 1980, C. Russell Nickel became executive director of FCSI, moving the organization's headquarters to Nickel's Seattle office.

"Russ made us toe the line, developed real budgets, and simply managed our affairs properly," Eaton says of the move. Nickel also developed sponsorship programs for seminars and accepted some limited advertising within Society publications. The financial hemorrhage stopped and FCSI was able to turn attention back to improving the services offered by the organization and melding the cultures brought by the merger.

A Different Spirit

Although the members of the former FFCS had prided themselves on being the "pure" independent consultants working toward building a recognized profession, the ISFSC membership brought into the new FCSI two components which have changed the very nature of the Society.

First, ISFSC had been publishing a regular communications piece called *The Consultant*. Edited by Russ Nickel, *The Consultant* was more a professional journal than the *FFCS Spec Sheet* published by FFCS. *The Consultant* quickly became the professional publication of FCSI.[34]

"*The Consultant* was a very important part of the new organization and became a strong element to show our expertise and bring us recognition within the industry," says Bill Eaton.

Just as important as the professional journal was the international tradition and scope brought into FCSI by the ISFSC members. FFCS had a Canadian Chapter, but ISFSC had European members. In fact, ISFSC held a joint meeting in Barcelona prior to the merger.

"There was an international focus promoted by the ISFSC," says Eaton, who during his presidency, journeyed to Bern, Switzerland, to confer with a European group interested in forming a chapter.

Bruno Brivio, a central figure in the formation of the European Chapter of FCSI, clearly recalls those early days of outreach by first ISFSC, then FCSI. "In the early 1970s, I made a couple of study trips to the U.S.," says Brivio. While on one of his trips, Brivio came to know Harry Freidman, one of the early ISFSC pioneers. Brivio joined the group and soon Friedman urged him to form a European chapter.

"At first, I told Harry that was a crazy idea," Brivio says. "I was sure we had no more than ten or twelve people in Europe who would be interested." Brivio underestimated the potential response. After the merger, Brivio, together with European pioneers Peter Streuli and Leif Torné, organized a seminar in Switzerland and were amazed when more than seventy professionals from Switzerland and Germany attended.

---

[34] Whereas *The Consultant* became the professional publication, the *FFCS Spec Sheet* was renamed the *FCSI Spec Sheet*, and served as the quarterly news and information publication for FCSI members.

Trudi Bernard accepts the charter for the Canadian Chapter from President Bill Caruso at the 1984 meeting in Toronto.

From these modest organizing moves spearheaded by ISFSC, then further encouraged by FCSI, the international focus spread well beyond the founders' humble expectations.

Both the professional publication and the international outreach quickly became hallmarks of FCSI thanks to the ISFSC legacy.

Appealing to the Smallest Nations

Longtime FCSI member Leif Torné recalls that in those early years of the European Chapter the largest number of members came from two of the smallest nations.

"Switzerland and Sweden each had about five to seven members," Torné says. "We had one or two members from big countries like France, Spain, and England. About the same time as the European chapter started in 1972, the Swedish Society of Foodservice Consultants, SKBF (*Storkökskonsulternas Branschförening*) was formed," Torné recalls.

The SKBF was not directly related to FCSI (or ISFSC in those days). The equipment suppliers in Sweden had a well-functioning organization and wanted a counterpart among the foodservice consultants with which to discuss projects and joint ventures. There were quite a few independent foodservice consultants in Sweden, as it was a clearly recognized profession.

The beginning of the ISFSC/FCSI European chapter was timed judiciously as the consulting profession was in differing states of development in the different nations on the European continent.

Over the ensuing years, the larger European countries have become the major centers of FCSI membership. Torné sees the local units eventually formed by FCSI as beneficial.

"This has been a lucky development for our international Society," Torné says. "We have also seen local societies in some countries being turned into local units of FCSI. That was a big leap forward, but in smaller European countries, for example Sweden, this would not be easy due to the language barrier."

Today's growing internationalization of the foodservice consulting industry can trace its roots to the initial efforts by the pioneers

CONTINUING PROFESSIONAL GROWTH PROGRAM

FCSI is committed to education—and clients are looking for consultants who stay on the cutting edge. That is why all FCSI Professional members are required to accumulate thirty continuing education units (CEUs) over a three-year period. The three-year period begins and ends on the same day for every Professional Member.

There are many ways in which Professional Members are able to acquire CEUs. For example, CEUs are given for attending seminars and trade shows, writing articles, making presentations, and successfully completing modules of the FCSI Professional Competency Exam. This is just one more way FCSI puts value in the "FCSI" initials after Professional members' names.

in Europe during the 1970s who were willing to work together to convince the North Americans of the truly global nature of the work. They also toiled relentlessly to show the Americans that there was much more to learn in the global economy. Those lessons would eventually pay off during the 1990s.

Moving Forward

With Russ Nickel's guidance, FCSI moved steadily towards increasing membership and solidifying the gains achieved by the merger.

In 1980, the traditional Fall Seminar was moved from New York to Miami, Florida, where FCSI members met and conferred with representatives from the School of Hospitality Management of Florida International University. That same year, FCSI opened a secondary mailing address in Washington, D.C., which served as a base for potential future presence near legislative decision-makers as well as the leadership of many allied professional organizations.

Annual FCSI meetings were now much larger affairs, given the virtual doubling in membership rolls following the merger. By 1981, more than 170 attended seminars alone at the Annual Meeting held in May in Chicago. That year, FCSI started a notable tradition by inaugurating the "FCSI Council of Fellows." Begun as a means to honor and recognize specific Society members for their long years of service to the hospitality industry and the foodservice consulting profession, the first-ever inductees were Fred Schmid and Richard Flambert.

The recipients were inducted at the Annual Banquet and were given awards certificates and specially commissioned medallions as symbols of the organization's respect and appreciation for their efforts.

The growing internationalization of the Society was clearly apparent in the early 1980s, as Bruno Brivio of Switzerland and Juan Prieto of Mexico were elected to the FCSI Board of Directors for 1981–1982.

Richard Flambert (left) and Fred Schmid were the first inductees into the prestigious FCSI Council of Fellows.

Growing in Influence and Members

The 1980s became a time of quiet but increasing professionalism for FCSI membership. One of the areas that benefited members and increased the Society's reputation was in expanded workshops and seminars.

"We developed a reputation for quality within our seminars," says Russ Nickel about those years following the historic merger. "Word got around and we developed a good working relationship with some of the other trade organizations who supported the meetings," Nickel adds.[35]

The interest in the information programs attracted members, so during this period FCSI formed and promoted the expansion of regional chapters. "We began to spread our wings," Nickel says of the time when FCSI was enlarged from two chapters to twelve in a decade.

Two nagging philosophical issues again concerned FCSI members during the early 1980s. Both of them were related to the relationship

---

[35] Russ Nickel wrote in the summer 1983 issue of *The Consultant* that the Society's growing reputation was such that a foodservice consultant from Australia had traveled to the 1983 National Restaurant Association Convention in Chicago, expressly to attend the FCSI seminars, and not simply to attend NRA. The consultant, Alan Felton, subsequently applied for FCSI membership based on the Society's reputation for education and useful programs.

Robert Kaiser served as the final ISFSC president and was closely involved in FCSI merger efforts. Kaiser has promoted a broader recognition of operational consultants in the foodservice industry.

between consultants and manufacturers. Although manufacturer-associated consultants already members of ISFSC were grandfathered into the new FCSI, the Society specifically denied future members with such relationships. Unfortunately, there were several consultants at that time who received payments from manufacturers for recommending their products in design installations.

Although such activity was prohibited in the Society's Code of Ethics, the Society (because of federal government policies) found it increasingly difficult, if not impossible, to enforce the Code. Rulings by the Federal Trade Commission and the Department of Justice against other professional organizations made punitive actions based on a Code of Ethics far more unlikely to be upheld.

Other organizations moved towards a "voluntary" Code. Within FCSI, the leadership used publications to decry unethical practices, while at the same time studying the potential viability of an FCSI registration or certification program.

While the feasibility of certification was being studied by the Society, the organization went on record calling for the "total elimination of payments" to consultants by manufacturers.

By 1984, FCSI's Board unveiled a "Certification/Professional Development Program," designed to codify and qualify members while hopefully eventually eliminating the thorny problems associated with such payments.

Moving to "The Next Level"

When William Caruso took over the mantle as FCSI president in 1984, the earliest growing pains of the combined FCSI seemed finally to have subsided. The leadership of the Society now poised the organization to move beyond the birth phase and begin the needed reforms and tasks for a basic stabilization. Merging of any entities is never easy. Organizational culture clashes are inevitable. However, the good will of members prevailed and by the mid-1980s, FCSI was well on its way to a new prominence.

"We have discarded the basic 'existence' priorities that were once paramount to our survival and are now embarking on fine tuning what we've developed—in short, setting our sights on new horizons," FCSI President Caruso told the members in the summer of 1984.[36]

Caruso cited the new liability and medical insurance programs and original marketing efforts as two of the many tangible enhancements offered to members.[37]

The hard work and stabilization apparently paid off in a big way for FCSI. By 1985, the Society's membership had grown to 540—dramatically up from the fewer than 300 members recorded following the 1979 merger.[38]

As the organization observed the thirtieth anniversary of the founding of FFES in 1985, FCSI members stood ready to grapple with the issues of the future. In 1985, those considerations included: organizational strategic planning, growing internationalism, the increased formation of regional and local chapters, and the movement towards professional certification of members in their field.

By the time Ronald Kooser was FCSI president in 1983, the Society had improved revenue flow from sponsorships and workshop fees so that the annual organizational operating budget depended on less than half of its income from dues.

---

[36] Remarks taken from the "President's Letter" in the summer 1984 issue of *The Consultant*, p. 2.

[37] Fiscally, FCSI had come a long way from the financial precipice it had almost fallen over in 1980. By 1983, the Society had managed to pare its budgetary reliance upon dues to 47 percent of the total organizational revenue. Thanks to the hard work of the Board as administered through Executive Director Russ Nickel, the revenue stream from sponsors, seminar income, and investments had grown dramatically, much to the membership's benefit.

[38] And a far cry from the fourteen Charter Members at the 1955 formation of FFES.

In 1985, FCSI Board Members conducted the first seminar in Mexico.

The strategic planning initiative resulted in the development of FCSI's Mission Statement: *To promote professionalism in foodservice/ hospitality and to prudently develop and efficiently manage a quality association within a budget that returns maximum benefits to all members.*

Major Changes

In 1986, FCSI boasted six hundred members, thirty-two of whom were in Europe. That year, FCSI planned to hold its first Fall Seminar outside of the United States. Unfortunately, the meeting, scheduled to be held in Paris in conjunction with a hotel trade show, was cancelled due to the threat of terrorist bombings.[39] The European chapter went ahead and met at the Paris show without incident.[40]

---

[39] Russ Nickel reports that the proposed Paris seminar was ironically the only event for which he had purchased event cancellation insurance. After a protracted period of negotiations with the insurance carrier, FCSI was reimbursed for virtually all expenses involved.

[40] According to Nicolas Elshof, a delegation of Canadian FCSI members, led by Trudy Bernard, attended the meeting along with many FCSI affiliate members, resulting in a successful event despite the ongoing fears.

With the growth in numbers and geographic spread, the Board moved to make structural changes to better serve the changing needs of the members.

FCSI and its predecessors, FFES and ISFSC, had met in conjunction with the National Restaurant Association Convention, held each year in Chicago in May. FFES was founded during the 1955 NRA show at the Drake Hotel in Chicago. FFES, and then FCSI, had established the tradition of holding the Society's major event, the Annual Meeting, as part of the Chicago NRA gathering.

By the 1980s, however, many FCSI members actually preferred attending the NAFEM (The National Association of Food Equipment Manufacturers) show, held in the fall every other year[41] in different cities. As an experiment, FCSI organized the Fall Meetings in conjunction with NAFEM in 1983 and 1985.

For those members with limited travel and convention budgets, more and more were opting to attend only the Fall Meeting, passing up the traditional Chicago Annual Meeting. In response to this changing marketplace, the FCSI Board decided to switch gears in 1987.

The Annual Meeting would now be moved from the May NRA show in Chicago to the fall. The Annual Meeting was traditionally the largest and most wide-ranging of FCSI's events, featuring the broadest number of seminars and workshops. The Annual Meeting, renamed "The Annual Seminar" would be held in conjunction with the NAFEM show in odd years, and for the first time ever, the FCSI Annual Seminar would be a completely stand-alone event in the fall of even years, when the NAFEM show was not being held.

When Bill Caruso took over as FCSI president in 1984, the majority of the "merger pains" were past and the Society stepped up to an even higher level of professional service to its members.

---

[41] NAFEM was held in "odd" calendar years—1983, 1985, 1987, etc.

Mike Stack was president from 1986 to 1987.

The Fall Annual Seminar would now rotate among cities, as did NAFEM.

What had been the Fall Meeting, was now renamed the Mini-Seminar, and each year that event would take place in conjunction with NRA in Chicago.

Bold Initiatives

By 1988, FCSI and its leadership team were deeply involved in broad issues involving the foodservice industry. Among them was growing support for a nationwide consolidated and consistent health and sanitation code. The growing disparity between state-supervised codes became an increasing source of confusion and contradiction. During this period, FCSI joined with other professional organizations in an attempt to standardize the multifaceted codes.

At the same time, FCSI began development of the Society's "Guide to Professional Practice and Operations,"[42] a useful and detailed publication designed to assist consultants in establishing the basics of their operations. When completed the guide would present information helpful in business operations, covering topics such as finances, personnel, marketing, production, and administration of consulting practices.

Part of this same initiative included the development of consistent instruments for FCSI members to use in recording and billing client time by firm members and a more standardized system for estimating fees for the purpose of assembling budgets.

Greater emphasis was given to the establishment of FCSI Chapters as well. By late 1987, the European, Canadian, Mexican, and New

---

[42] The resulting publication would eventually be called the *FCSI Manual of Professional Practice*.

England chapters were joined by a Southern California chapter. FCSI leadership aggressively promoted further chapter creation as a means for local professionals in the foodservice consulting industry to meet more frequently, to share information on industry trends and developments, and to provide a more regular framework for the sharing of expertise.

During the late 1980s, Thomas Costello worked hard to convince the Board and general membership to become more welcoming to management consultants within the foodservice industry. That outreach became Management Advisory Services and Costello edited a regular publication titled Critical MAS, which helped to explain to the designer consultants the work and importance of the management consultants.

By 1992, at the Phoenix Conference, a few of the seminars were produced for and by MAS consultants and ever since, there has been an educational track in each conference pertaining to this area of foodservice specialization.

Countering American Provincialism

As FCSI and its members headed into the closing years of the 1980s, the Society continued to turn more and more towards regionalization and internationalization.

Ceremonial presentation of the charter to the FCSI Mexico Chapter. From left: Hugo Garin, Bill Caruso, Juan Prieto, and Steve Marshall.

Salvatore Romano became FCSI president in 1990.

Not that the circumstances for the Europeans was all that easy or equitable. Part of the task was the need to alter the North American perspective.

"One of the biggest problems in those years was getting the members to open their eyes and look abroad," says Bruno Brivio. The European members worked very hard to convince all the members "that the world is bigger than the U.S. and Canada," Brivio notes.

British FCSI pioneer Hugh Cade echoes Brivio's sentiments. "Being a member of FCSI in those days was an act of faith. American foodservice was seen as something to look up to, so even though we attended conferences with those who were primarily Americans, we did learn a lot about what was going on in the world of foodservice," Cade adds.

Brivio, Cade,[43] and Nicolas Elshof, together with their European colleagues relentlessly presented a more cosmopolitan perspective, eventually turning the worldview of the entire organization into a truly international endeavor.

"It was a struggle," Cade says of that time period. "But now I think a majority of people see FCSI as a worldwide organization. It is one of the few organizations that is truly a worldwide Society."

"For several years at that time FCSI's European chapter had some difficulty attracting more European members into the Society," says FCSI European pioneer and visionary Nicolas Elshof.

In 1988, when Elshof became chairman of the European chapter he notified the Board of Directors that the $3,000 per year then being

---

[43] Hugh Cade served as president of FCSI from September 1998 to September 1999.

given by the Board was not enough to create a clear FCSI identity in Europe. Elshof recommended that European members pay their membership fees directly to FCSI Europe instead of sending the funds back to FCSI headquarters in Seattle.

"That way we could play the value of the dollar," Elshof says. By doing so, more money was left in the European FCSI account. But the Board also increased the annual contribution to the European chapter to $10,000.

With the increase in funding, the first task was to create a European identity. "Bruno Brivio gave us a helping hand and his secretary, Alice Arnold, became our part-time executive secretary," Elshof says. With that move, FCSI Europe had local direction, an office in Zurich, and was ready to promote FCSI in Europe.

By the end of Elshof's term, there were more than ninety FCSI European members and the budget grew to more than $50,000. With the spirited growth in numbers, the European members began to lobby aggressively for a more truly international scope to FCSI.

A Firestorm Erupts over a Plan

In January 1989, Elshof developed a plan he called "FCSI Keep on Rolling." Essentially a vision for the future, Elshof's plan presented a cosmopolitan perspective of FCSI. The European chapter adopted the plan and presented the proposal to the FCSI Board of Directors at the 1989 Fall Seminar as a basis for international restructuring.

Initially, the "Keep on Rolling" plan was given scant attention, however the Board was unprepared for the emotional response on the part of the European members.

Fred Schmid mentored many foodservice consultants, among them Tony Clevenger.

"We were furious!" Elshof contends about the brush-off. "We were emotional because we realized that this was very important for the future of FCSI. If the Board of Directors would not listen to our plan, it could have meant the end of FCSI in Europe," Elshof says.

Luckily, John Birchfield, Sr., then-president of FCSI, listened to the European delegates and asked the full Board of Trustees to present that plan immediately to the Board of Directors.

"His actions saved FCSI from a disaster." Elshof adds. The Europeans now at least had the attention of the North Americans and constructive discussions regarding the proposal continued for the next several years.

In 1992, Elshof and Bob Pacifico shared a taxi to the Zurich airport, and on the way, Elshof contends that Pacifico inquired as to why it was so important for FCSI Europe to have the "Keep on Rolling" plan adopted by FCSI Worldwide.

Elshof explained that it was critical that operating divisions should be created within FCSI so that all local members could have a feeling of equality and rights within FCSI. Convinced of the importance,

From left: John Birchfield and Sam Crabtree with H. G. "Gene" Rice during Rice's induction into the Council of Fellows in 1989.

FCSI president Mike Colburn (right) presents Mike Johnson of Atlanta with the 1988 Charter recognizing the formation of the Southeast Chapter.

Pacifico and other North American colleagues successfully lobbied for the plan's adoption.

With these events, FCSI Europe became the first Division of FCSI.[44]

Changing Attitudes

Hugh Cade played a particularly significant role in the overall development of FCSI UK. Cade was a member of the Society of Catering and Hotel Management Consultants (SCHMC), a similar organization founded in Britain in the 1960s. As Cade and other countrymen became more active in FCSI, they considered merging the two tiny groups.

Cade says that in the 1980s, there were only four or five FCSI members in the UK, and the SCHMC had perhaps twenty to thirty. They were both struggling. "I gave a presentation suggesting that we merge SCHMC and FCSI to form the local UK unit of FCSI," Cade

---

[44] In 1996 when Hugh Cade became chairman of FCSI Europe he broadened the idea of "Keep on Rolling," creating local units. The first local unit was FCSI Nederland, followed by FCSI UK, FCSI Switzerland, and later on FCSI France and FCSI Germany.

From left: Jim Little, Juan Prieto, Bill Eaton, John Fellers, Murray Perl, Charlie Wood, and Bill Caruso.

Leif Torné was one of several European foodservice consulting professionals who spearheaded the development of the European Chapter.

says. Although the organization members looked with favor on the idea, there was, however, the ingrained American-centered mindset to overcome.

"When I first became involved in the [FCSI] governance in Europe, the Americans used to send someone over to sort of 'beat us up' and tell us what we couldn't do," Cade recalls. "It was only in the early 1990s when people like Michael Johnson and Bob Pacifico and others saw that there was a world outside of North America. They also saw the importance of not treating people outside North America as a nuisance, but in fact realizing that they were very much part of the future of the Society," Cade says with candor.

Eventually, Cade rallied support from all sectors and the merger of SCHMC into FCSI took place in 1996–1997. By 1999, the merged group formed FCSI UK, which quickly became the largest local unit in Europe with Germany close behind.

Current FCSI President Ken Winch adds that a similar group in Germany, B.I.G.,[45] joined FCSI in 1999 to form FCSI Germany (now FCSI Germany-Austria). The Affiliation Agreement between FCSI Europe and FCSI Germany was signed in January 2000.

Gerhard Franzen recalls that the B.I.G. members chose to join FCSI because of the organization's growing international focus, the real network the association provided, the professional management behind FCSI, as well as the expanded organizational identity.

As FCSI and its membership moved into the 1990s, the organization had come together and proved the worth of unity. However, the Society was soon poised at a crossroad, which required several decisions—some of them painful. Once made, FCSI would move to a higher level of professionalism. By the end of the century, FCSI would look and be run very differently from the small organization of colleagues started by Fred Schmid in 1955. ■

---

[45] B.I.G. is the German acronym for *Berater im Gastgewerbe*, which in English is "Consultants in the Foodservice Industry."

In 1983, FCSI President Murray Perl presented a Presidential Citation to Phil Young of MAFSI. FCSI members Ira Beer (left) and George Kraft (right) looked on.

MEMBER CATEGORIES AND QUALIFICATIONS

Classes of Members

The Society shall have four primary classes of members: Consultant Members, Allied Members, Affiliate Members, and Student Members.

Consultant Members

The Society shall have two categories of Consultant Members: Individual Members and Consulting Firm Members. All Consultant Members shall abide by the Consultant Member Code of Conduct.

Individual Consultant Members

Individual Consultant membership, with the exception of Emeritus and Student Members, is limited to individuals whose main employment is in a capacity typically associated with consulting activities.

Consultant qualifications, rights, and privileges for each individual consultant membership classification are as follows:

Professional Member Qualifications

a. Shall demonstrate a high level of competence in and knowledge of the following:

—*The Foodservice and Hospitality Industry*
—*Consulting Assignment Management*
—*Professional Specialism*
—*Business Management*
—*FCSI Code of Conduct*

The Board of Directors shall from time to time, and following consultation with Consultant Members, determine and publish what constitutes these competency and knowledge requirements and standards.

b. Shall have been active as a consultant with assignment management responsibility for a minimum of two years.

c. Shall have provided satisfactory references from a minimum of three clients.

d. Shall have been supported in their application by two existing Professional Members (not being their employer, employee or partner). This support may either take the form of references from members with knowledge of the applicant or by interview.

e. Shall fulfill continuing professional growth requirements, as set forth by the Board of Examiners and approved by the Board of Directors.

f. Shall comply with the FCSI Code of Conduct.

Rights and Privileges

a. Professional Members shall have the right to use the initials "FCSI" after their name.

b. Professional Members shall have the right to vote on issues requiring a membership vote.

c. Professional Members shall have the right to serve as an Officer and Director.

Senior Associate Member

a. Shall demonstrate the required level of competence in and knowledge of the following

—*The Foodservice and Hospitality Industry*
—*Consulting assignment management*
—*Professional Specialism*
—*Business Management*
—*FCSI Code of Conduct*

The Board of Directors shall from time to time, and following consultation with Consultant Members, determine and publish what constitutes these competency and knowledge requirements and standards.

b. Shall have been active as a consultant with assignment management responsibility for a minimum of one year.

c. Shall have provided satisfactory references from a minimum of two clients.

d. Shall have been supported in their application by two existing Professional Members (not being their employer, employee or partner). This support may either take the form of references from members with knowledge of the applicant or by interview.

e. Shall comply with the FCSI Code of Conduct.

Rights and Privileges

Senior Associate Members shall have the right to vote on issues requiring a membership vote. They shall not have the right to serve as an Officer or Director.

Associate Member
Qualifications
Currently employed in a capacity that can serve as partial qualification for more advanced membership. Shall comply with the FCSI Code of Conduct.

Rights and Privileges
Associate Members may not vote or serve as an Officer or Director.

Emeritus Member
Qualifications
Professional Member who has retired from active practice and no longer is involved, in any way, in the sale of projects through his or her personal intervention. An Emeritus Member may not solicit business, or in any way attend presentations in the active pursuit of commissions for himself/herself or any firm.

Rights and Privileges
Emeritus Members may use the designation "FCSI Emeritus." They shall not have the right to vote or serve as an Officer or Director.

Consulting Firm Members
Consulting Firm membership is only available to those organizations that practice consulting as a significant line of business and are totally independent of any equipment or other supply or facilities operation or management organization. A Consulting Firm Member must be owned by or employ in a senior management position at least one Professional Consultant Member and as a firm must carry out its business in line with the FCSI Code of Conduct.

Rights and Privileges
a. Only Consulting Firm Members may use the FCSI logo on their published materials; and

b. May incorporate the following wording in their published materials "A consulting firm regulated by FCSI and subscribing to the FCSI Code of Conduct"; and

c. Only Consulting Firm Members may be listed in Society publications aimed at clients.

d. Consulting Firm Members may not vote.

Allied Members
There shall be two categories of Allied Member: Individual and Corporate Member. Allied membership classes are available to companies and individuals that are in foodservice/hospitality related businesses and that express an interest in the issues, information, and associations common to the foodservice/hospitality consulting field. Allied Members may not vote. Allied Members may serve as a Director but not as an Officer.

Corporate Member
   Qualifications

   Must be allied with the Foodservice/Hospitality Industry and evidence a desire to affiliate with FCSI in its stated objectives.

   Corporate Members may designate two individuals as the Corporate Member Representatives.

Individual Member
   Qualifications

   Individual Members must be allied with the Foodservice/Hospitality Industry and evidence a desire to affiliate with FCSI in its stated objectives.

Affiliate Members

   Affiliate membership is available to companies and individuals that operate, manage, or provide professional services or education relating to the management of foodservice or hospitality facilities. Affiliate Members shall not have the right to vote or serve as an Officer.

Student Members

Student membership is available to students attending an accredited institution of higher learning and enrolled in a foodservice or hospitality related course of study. Student Members shall not have the right to vote or serve as an Officer or Director.

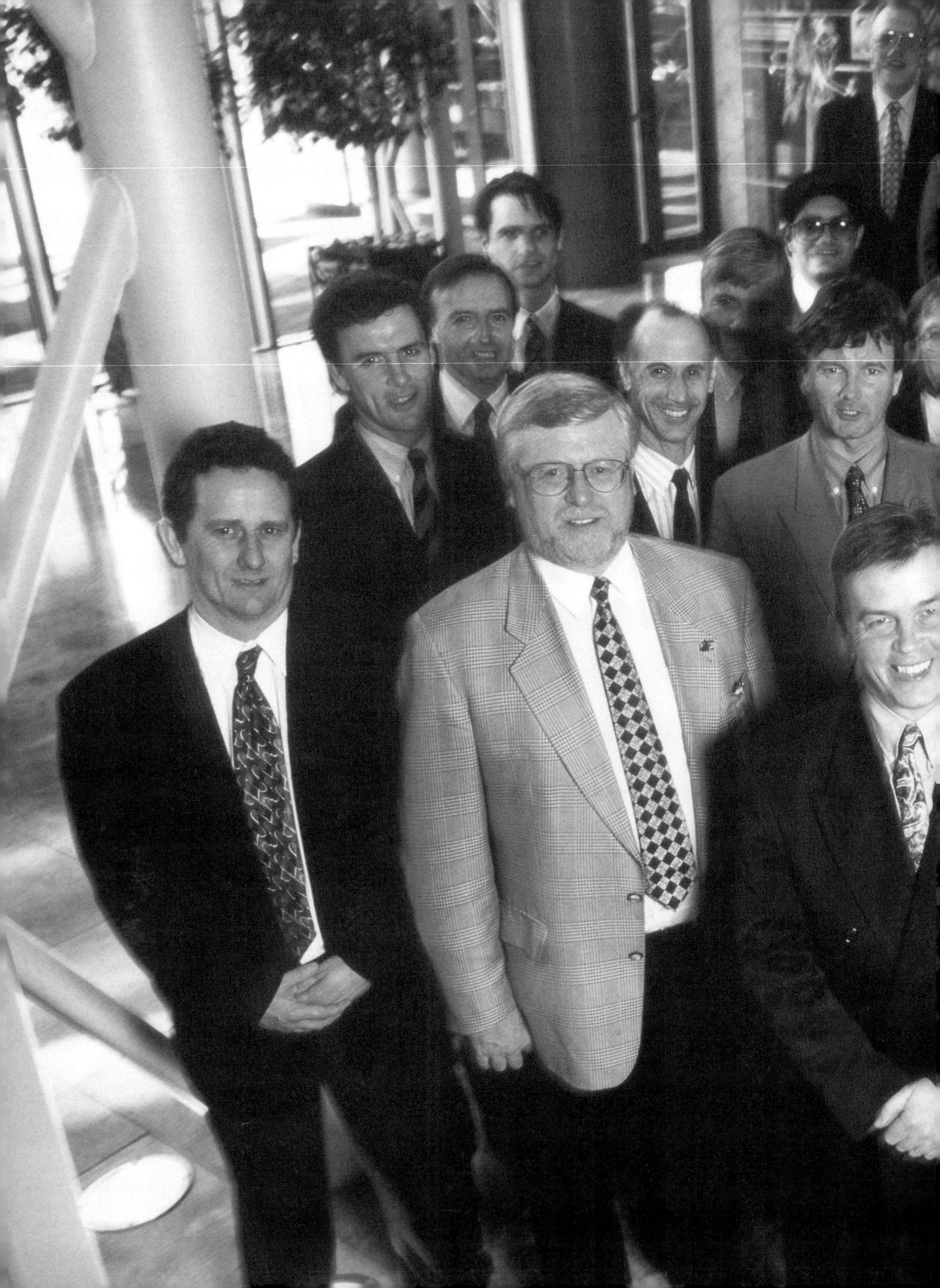

4

"Ours is one of few organizations that is truly worldwide…"

—Hugh R. Cade, FCSI president 1998–1999

Worldwide Presence

The members of the Foodservice Consultants Society International grappled with several major issues as the world community witnessed the end of one century and ventured into the next. By the time the membership would turn that calendar page, the changes in FCSI would be amazing...

"As you confront any major change, you wonder if it is the right thing to do," says Tom Costello, FCSI president in 1992. "But you try to develop a vision for what will be better for the organization. It was like steering a ship through some very tough times," Costello says.

FCSI had come to a crossroads. The membership had increased steadily and grandly since the 1979 merger of FFCS and ISFSC. The quality of service and breadth of programs had increased dramatically. The chapter structure was established and flourishing.

Yet, still there was a great deal more to be done to propel the Foodservice Consultants Society International into the highest ranks of truly professional and influential international organizations.

Under New Management

In 1991, the FCSI Board began to grapple with issues related to how the organization was administered. Since 1980, FCSI had been capably and admirably overseen by Russ Nickel, who provided a high level of in-house management. Nickel's work had placed FCSI in sound financial footing following the disappointing experiment with outside professional management chosen immediately following the merger.

But in late 1991, the FCSI Board decided to once again place the operations of the Society into the hands of a professional association membership management company.

In October 1991, FCSI ended its relationship with Russ Nickel. Then-President Sal Romano, together with President-Elect Tom Costello and the Board of Directors, made the painful decision.

The Board reviewed the Society's options and decided that FCSI turn to a professional management firm with strong ties to the foodservice industry. Food Service Associates (FSA), headed by Philip Cooke, had been providing publications, editorial, and management services to foodservice-related organizations since 1969. In 1974, Cooke added professional management assistance

Pictured on pages 44–45:
FCSI UK formed in 1999, boosted by the merger of the Society of Catering and Hotel Management Consultants (SCHMC) into FCSI that took place in 1996–1997.

Opposite:
Nicolas Elshof was one of the early visionaries who propelled the at-times reluctant FCSI membership to think of its role as a global one.

to an organization, which eventually became the Society for Foodservice Management. Cooke was well known to many of FCSI members and proceeded to orchestrate a seamless transition in mid-1992.

During an interim period, FCSI was administered by Gudrun Roehrenbeck, who served as acting executive director and editor of *The Consultant*. During the transitional few months, Roehrenbeck supervised the movement of *The Consultant* completely in-house, with all editorial functions, layout, and design now performed by FCSI management staff. The move immediately saved the Society a considerable amount of money.

Phyllis Ann Marshall presented one of the management advisory seminars at the 1992 conference in Phoenix.

Another Move

Gudrun Roehrenbeck supervised the transition until Cooke and FSA formally took over the reins in June 1992. The handover resulted in another move for the FCSI headquarters, as the records and files kept by Russ Nickel in his Seattle offices were now transported to FSA's offices in Louisville.

FCSI was now administered by a much larger management organization than before.[46] The cross-cultural interplay of ideas among the many foodservice-related professional and trade organizations could only be of benefit to FCSI members.

Philip Cooke assumed the title of FCSI executive vice president and promptly began providing an expanded range of services to the Society.

---

[46] FCSI was in good company, since at the time FSA began management services in June 1992, the firm was providing similar assistance for the Society for Foodservice Management, the International Association of Culinary Professionals, the National Association of Catering Executives, the Inflight Food Service Association, and the Foodservice Coalition for a Better Environment.

To assist in supervising the day-to-day minutiae of FCSI membership needs, Cooke hired David L. Drain, a recent graduate of Abilene Christian University who had background in foodservice and a degree in marketing. Drain and Cooke took over the records, membership information, and financial administration of FCSI, which had grown to seven hundred members by 1992.

"Our first task was to take the organization to a higher level of professionalism," Drain recalls. FSA immediately began producing monthly financial statements, integrating more computer technology into Society recordkeeping, and orchestrating the annual conference and regional seminars.

FCSI EDUCATIONAL FOUNDATION

In 1995, FCSI members moved their concern for the future of the profession to a higher level by establishing the Foodservice Consultants Society International Educational Foundation. Established as an independent entity separate from FCSI, the foundation is a nonprofit corporation dedicated to furthering education in the foodservice consulting industry.

The FCSI Educational Foundation works to benefit the FCSI membership as well as the general public. Overseen by an independent Board of Directors, the foundation works towards its goals through funding scholarships, student attendance at the FCSI Annual Conference, research projects, and involvement in foodservice consulting issues.

A special Student Section of the foundation provides assistance in application for scholarship applications and internship opportunities. An annual essay contest provides winners with an all-expense paid trip to an FCSI Annual Conference or other industry event.

The FCSI Educational Foundation is funded through contributions, endowments, bequests, and gifts from FCSI members, corporate friends, and members of the general public interested in furthering foodservice consulting education. Specific fund-raising events host silent auctions held at the FCSI Annual Conference and regional special events.

The first big test came in fall 1992 at the FCSI Annual Seminar, which was held at the Arizona Biltmore in Phoenix. After a few years in which membership attendance at meetings and seminars had dwindled, "Attendees unanimously agreed that this was the best ever in all respects," said then-FCSI President Carl Vail. FSA, Cooke and Drain had passed an important initial milestone.

An immediate benefit apparent to the Board and general membership was the impact of FSA's interrelationship with other foodservice organizations.

"The contacts that Phillip had and the people he knew proved invaluable to the organization," Drain says. Another benefit to FCSI was the improved financial condition. The Society ended 1992 with a surplus, after struggling in recent years.

Strategic Alliances

In 1993, FCSI's Board moved to establish much closer working relationships with several client-based associations in the industry. Beginning at the fall 1993 Annual Seminar in New Orleans, FCSI

The support of sponsors helped FCSI increase the caliber of its meetings.

Sal Romano, John Cini, Charlie Wood, and Ron Kooser at Sal Romano's induction ceremony into the Fellows in 1993.

established liaison committees to work closely with the American Correctional Food Service Association (ACFSA), the American School Food Service Association (ASFSA), the National Association of College and University Food Services (NACUFS), and the Society for Foodservice Management (SFM).

Starting in 1994, FCSI began offering member talents to these and other organizations, including menu planning, employee training, conceptual design services, facilities planning, and a speakers' clearing house.

The underlying purpose of this initiative was to further increase awareness of FCSI within these realms, while offering additional opportunities for FCSI members to provide professional services.

During this time, FCSI changed its bylaws to permit suppliers to join the organization, instituting the new membership category of "Allied Members." Previously, suppliers had been termed "Patrons" and their names listed in a special section of *The Consultant*. The "Patrons" had paid a fee to be so listed and upon

President Carl Vail thanks Brian Sill (left) for chairing the 1993 conference in New Orleans.

Tassos Kioulpapas was chair of FCSI Europe from 1992 to 1995.

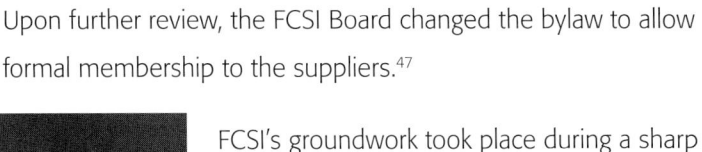

review by the Internal Revenue Service during an organization audit, this circumstance was seen to be a violation of IRS rules as they pertained to what was deemed "advertising" in a nonprofit organization's publication.

Upon further review, the FCSI Board changed the bylaw to allow formal membership to the suppliers.[47]

FCSI's groundwork took place during a sharp economic recession in the early 1990s. Building, construction, and renovations of food facilities during the period was virtually "on hold," as companies and institutions guarded their shrinking available financial resources and postponed major building and remodeling projects. FCSI members experienced a related downturn in their own business as a result. The Board's efforts to promote these new

---

[47] The first Allied Member to be elected to the FCSI Board of Directors took place in September 1996, as Rod Collins joined the directors with full voting privileges.

relationships and alliances would pay off as the economy turned up in the mid-1990s.

Few were prepared or could predict how strongly the economy would rebound, however. The balance of the final decade of the century saw significant economic expansion. By mid-1994, that expansion was well underway and FCSI members benefited from the new round of construction and remodeling of foodservice facilities across the globe.

Also during Bob Pacifico's term as president, the FCSI Board authorized the creation of the FCSI Educational Foundation as a separate, not-for-profit, charitable organization. Originally envisioned as an agency to fund scholarships for students entering the foodservice consulting profession, the Foundation refocused its goals to underwrite traditional educational programming to directly enhance member and industry expectations.

Chapter leaders from the late 1980s. Standing from left: Mike Johnson, unidentified, Bob Pacifico, Jim Petersen, Ed Ludemann, Juan Prieto, Jose Gomez, Karl Heinz Kreuzig, and Bob Schmid. Seated from left: Nelson Hofer, Helen Baxter, and Larry Dubov.

Editorial Changes

To meet the new challenges of the heated 1990s, FSA moved to change the look and editorial nature of *The Consultant*, long-established as the professional journal of FCSI.

"In 1994, we overhauled *The Consultant* magazine," says David Drain about what was seen as a significant change. The publication had been a black-and-white, fairly staid magazine. FSA revamped the look, adding full color, and for the first time, accepting advertising in order to underwrite the considerable expense of the now slick professional periodical.

The FCSI Board entrusted FSA staff with a great amount of responsibility for producing *The Consultant*, Drain says. "We set the editorial direction and graphic design and solicited member input," Drain adds. Slowly, *The Consultant* grew from a somewhat modest size to a hefty publication with many more pages thanks to the use

Bill Marvin (left) and Tom Costello proudly display books each had published.

Nicole Wyss, chair of the European Conference in Paris in 1992 and FCSI President Carl Vail.

of four-color inks throughout and the addition of a great amount of advertising.

The editorial transformation taking place in *The Consultant* mirrored the changes taking place within FCSI and how it was run and perceived. The increased revenue as a result of advertising in *The Consultant* provided an income stream for FCSI to embark on ventures otherwise financially impossible. Two initiatives undertaken included further internationalization and attention to the worldwide impact of FCSI, and allied with that, additional support staff to provide the services of a truly worldwide professional Society.

FCSI Asia Pacific

Thanks to the initiative shown by Sal Romano and the vision developed by Nicolas Elshof, by 1994 and 1995 the FCSI European division was flourishing. However, other sections of the globe were now becoming active and important Society members, clamoring for attention as the Europeans had done for more than a decade.

At the FCSI Europe Board meeting in Zurich in 1995. From left: Hugh Cade, Tassos Kioulpapas, Garry Nokes, Ken Winch, Alice Arnold, Kathleen Seelye, David Drain, Veronique Najar-Giroud, Nicolas Elshof, Bob Pacifico, Barbara Hohmann-Beck, and Phillip Cooke.

FCSI ADMINISTRATORS OVER THE YEARS

Since 1992, FCSI has enjoyed professional administration through the experienced firm of FSA Group (formerly known as Food Service Associates). Over the organization's history, however, the crucial day-to-day operations, including member services, dues, publications, and event planning, have been handled in different ways.

In the early years, more often than not, the organization's president would perform many of the duties, no doubt relying whenever possible upon his company's support staff (if there were any) for carrying out the "nuts-and-bolts" tasks of organization administration.

As FCSI grew in members and sophistication, executive directors were hired as full-time employees. Eventually, staff was added as well as office space and information storage. Today's fast-paced and information-led society and culture demands "cutting edge" professional administration to organize the many facets of FCSI's member services. The old adage "the buck stops here," however, has always applied and the following is the listing of those who have filled the role of head of organization:

1955–1956	(FFES President Fred Schmid and his company staff provided member services until the organization could support an executive secretary)
1956–1962	Murl M. Schull, executive secretary (Schull was an employee of Fred Schmid who provided the services to the organization at no salary)
1963–1971	Arthur B. Olian, executive secretary (Olian was FCSI's first paid employee)
1972–1973	Ellis Murphy, executive secretary
1973–1978	Henry Rothman, executive director
1978–1979	Ronald C. Hunt, executive director
1979–1980	Jerry R. Patterson, executive director
1980–1991	C. Russell Nickel, executive director (and later, executive vice president)
1991–1992	Gudrun Roehrenbeck, acting executive director
1992–2001	Philip S. Cooke, executive vice president
2002–present	David Drain, executive vice president

FCSI members at the Western Restaurant Show in Los Angeles in 1993. From left: Don Avalier, Tom Costello, Stan Abrams, and Ira Spilky.

One of the first outreach activities beyond Europe took place in October 1994, as FCSI planned and staged one of the Society's "Problem-Solving Clinics"[48] in conjunction with the International Hospitality Show in Bangkok, Thailand. FCSI members from all of Asia and the "Pan-Pacific" region were targeted and invited to this breakthrough gathering.

FCSI Executive Vice President Philip Cooke used the opportunity to invite the interested members in the region to a special meeting the following year. That gathering, a breakfast meeting held in Hong Kong during the Hotel and Food Exhibition (HOFEX) show, challenged the members to begin a regional organizing initiative. Manila's Imelda Silayan took up the suggestion and began organizing many of the industry leaders in the area. Working closely with Nani Labrador and Hong Kong's Vivien Choi-Cheung, the trio planned a "chapter launch" meeting and seminar, which was held at the

---

[48] The "Problem-Solving Clinics" were specific issue-oriented workshops, which had been initiated by the FCSI at the National Restaurant Association Convention several years before.

Shangri-La Hotel on Edsa, Mandaluyong, in Manila on August 5, 1995. The Asia Pacific Chapter was underway.

The meeting attracted almost one hundred attendees, which included organizers Yasuo Inoue and Shigeru Suzuki from Japan, Prim Jitcharoongphorn from Thailand, and Carol Chia from Singapore.

The success of the Asia-Pacific chapter encouraged Australian FCSI members to establish a chapter there.

Innovations

In 1995, Kathleen H. Seelye became the first female FCSI president. Her selection came at a time of innovation for the forty-year-old Society. With a membership now approaching the one thousand mark, Seelye and her Board immediately undertook extensive planning and visioning for the future of the Society.

"We decided early on that we were going to develop a ten-year picture of where we wanted to go," Seelye says of her work as president. "We developed an approach more focused on international roles through separate divisions in Europe and Asia so that the Society was not going to be viewed as purely a U.S.-based association," Seelye continued. The Board saw great potential in expansion of the Society's worldwide activities.

The Board also commissioned a broad needs assessment of all FCSI members to determine their individual wants and to chart the future direction of the organization. This first-ever assessment process would provide the basis for the Society's plans and structure into the new century about to dawn.

During this time, the FCSI Board was populated by increasing non-American representation. Hugh Cade was chairman of the European

Bob Pacifico.

Division, Barbara Hohmann Beck was the second representative from Europe, and Vivien Choi-Cheung served as a representative from Asian countries.

Technology impacted FCSI in dramatic ways during the same period. Teleconferencing was initiated as an electronic means for training and research programs to enhance professional growth of

FCSI HEADQUARTERS LOCATIONS OVER THE YEARS

1955–1963	8032 West Third Street Los Angeles, California
1963–1971	1517 North Second Street Harrisburg, Pennsylvania
1972–1973	600 South Michigan Avenue Chicago, Illinois
1973–1978	135 Glenlawn Avenue Sea Cliff, New York
1978–1980	1800 Pickwick Avenue Glenview, Illinois
1980–1983	1000 Connecticut Avenue NW, Suite 9 Washington, DC (During these three years, FCSI maintained two offices, one in the nation's capital and administrative offices in Seattle.)
1980–1985	13227 8th Avenue NW Seattle, Washington
1985–1992	12345 30th Avenue NE, Suite H Seattle, Washington
1992–present	304 West Liberty, Suite 201 Louisville, Kentucky

Russ Nickel and John Birchfield.

In 1995, Kathleen Seelye became the first female FCSI president.

the members. Simultaneously, FCSI unveiled the Society's Internet site, **www.fcsi.org**, which offered yet another marketing and public awareness arm for the organization, while at the same time offering a wider array of services to members online.

With FSA's assistance, FCSI expanded the number of "Problem-Solving Clinics" and educational programs, regional seminars, and workshops so that a greater number of members could benefit from the presentations, while at the same time affording nonmembers and prospective members more chances to experience the professional impact of the Society.

The transformation of FCSI caused the Board to revisit the organization's Mission Statement, which was somewhat simplified that year to read, *To promote professionalism in foodservice and hospitality consulting while returning maximum benefit to all members.*

After conducting a membership needs assessment, the Board developed a renewed set of objectives. Among them was a call to revisit an old idea which had not been brought to fruition—accreditation. Once again the Society embarked on a journey to standardize expectations of foodservice professionals.

Throughout 1996 and 1997, a special FCSI Certification Task Force examined the feasibility of certification for the foodservice profession.

When Brian Sill became the president of FCSI in September 1996, he and the Board oversaw a movement to rethink and realign the chapter structure. The end result would be to establish "divisions" representing a more equitable geographic international distribution of membership. By this time, the preponderance of American majority membership in FCSI had shrunk to around 60 percent. The hoped-for restructuring would go far to making the Society even more international in scope, thinking, and representation.

Alice Arnold served as FCSI Europe executive director for many years from her office in Switzerland.

The movement towards membership certification took another step to reality as the Board authorized the establishment of a "Board of Examiners." The evolving structure was adopted on a provisional basis, pending further review and presentation to the membership.

Gradual Restructuring

FCSI showed the world of professional associations just how "international" the Society was in 1998, when Hugh Cade, one of the founders of the United Kingdom "Local Unit"[49] became president of FCSI. The first non-North American to become president of the Society, Cade saw a significant change in the mindset of FCSI members during the 1990s. "In the 1990s, many more Americans were coming over to attend meetings in Europe and they saw that this was the way forward," Cade says. "They realized that people outside of North America were very much a part of the future of the Society."

---

[49] What had been called chapters before were now called "local units" if they were single-country related or "divisions" if they were multinational.

From left: David Drain, Imelda Silayan, Carol Chia, and Beryl Yuhas confer before the FCSI Asia Pacific Chapter meeting in Singapore in 1998.

In 1998, FCSI boasted of having members in thirty countries on five continents. What is even more impressive, given the diversity of people within the organization who come from many differing cultures and backgrounds, is the fact that every one of the Society's members subscribes to the same common aims and code of ethics.

In January 2000, the FCSI Worldwide Board of Directors held their first meeting outside of North America—in Amsterdam. The meeting took place in conjunction with the FCSI Europe Annual Conference. A major discussion point at the Board meeting was the creation of a North American Division, mirroring the move by the European Chapter almost ten years before into forming a European Division.

"The discussions about forming a North American Division actually began in 1999 as Michael Pantano was getting ready to assume the FCSI presidency," says current Executive Vice President David Drain. Pantano advocated planning for a time when membership from other nations would outnumber the American contingent. When Pantano was in office, he and the FCSI Worldwide Board formed a special task force to study the proposal.

Their recommendations, presented in 2000, received positive feedback and the Board voted to accept their proposals. Part of the plan included a restructuring of responsibilities to avoid unnecessary duplication. The Worldwide Board was reduced from eleven to seven members.[50] A new, eight-member North American Board of Trustees was formed, following the format of the European Division.

The inaugural North American Board of Trustees was elected in 2001 at the Orlando Conference held in September of that auspicious year.

At the same time, a general review of the FCSI bylaws had been conducted by another task force. After many years of changes and amendments, the bylaws had become a patchwork. Under Hugh Cade's leadership, the Bylaws Task Force analyzed the entire document and submitted a newly written set of bylaws, which reflected the changes that had taken place, yet maintained the original intent of the writers.

The new bylaws, presented in 2002, formally included the new North American Division and the revamped Worldwide Board. The structure formalized the Worldwide Board into a representative

---

[50] Accomplished through attrition.

Scott Legge and Garry Nokes at the 2002 Conference in Barcelona.

FCSI EUROPEAN CHAIRS

Christian Petzold
European Chapter chair, October 1972–October 1975

Leif Torné
European Chapter chair, October 1975–October 1978

Peter Streuli
European Chapter chair, October 1978–October 1981

Bruno Brivio
European Chapter chair, October 1981–October 1984

Oke Widgren
European Chapter chair, October 1984–October 1985

Karl-Heinz Kreuzig
European Chapter chair, October 1985–October 1988

Nicolas Elshof
European Chapter chair, October 1988–January 1992

Tassos Kioulpapas
European Division chair, January 1992–November 1995

Hugh Cade
European Division chair, November 1995–June 1998

Kenneth Winch
European Division chair, June 1998–April 2001

Gerhard Kühnel
European Division chair, April 2001–May 2005

Rosemary Osbourne
European Division chair, May 2005–Present

group of Directors that would include one European, two North Americans, one representative of the Non-Aligned membership (those not part of a Division), and three officers elected among the Board.

Toward Certification

Also during Pantano's term, the long-debated move towards FCSI certification took several steps closer to reality. And just as quickly, the membership stepped back again to consider the proposition a bit more. A special membership vote held in 2000, on the acceptance of mandatory Professional Member testing, failed by a very slim margin.

The proposal had been more than three years in the preparatory phase with a special task force of members working very hard to develop an equitable structure for the test. President Pantano noted in his regular column in *The Consultant* that a major factor in the initiative's defeat was the surprising volume of e-mail communications disseminated during the voting process, many containing commentary on issues that most thought had been equitably resolved through discussion and committee action.

Although the task force had submitted regular reports and updates, often seeking reaction and input from the membership, many members either voted against the proposal or simply did not vote at all, contributing to the defeat of the plan.

While the testing proposal failed, the members did approve a continuing education requirement. An interim Board of Examiners, originally established to oversee the proposed testing program, moved their attention toward what eventually became the FCSI Continuing Professional Growth Program.

Later in 2000, the Board of Examiners completed the FCSI Basic Competency Exam, which because of the defeat of the original testing proposal, was offered to the members as an optional activity worth continuing education units (CEUs).

Scott Legge and Tom Ricca congratulate Nicolas Elshof and Hugh Cade during their induction into the Council of Fellows in 2002.

A Change in Professional Managers

Philip Cooke and his management firm FSA continued to serve FCSI worldwide membership through the balance of the 1990s and into the first decade of the twenty-first century. During that span, Cooke served FCSI in the role of executive vice president.

As FCSI grew, particularly in the international sphere, Cooke turned increasingly to his assistant, David Drain, to tend to the day-to-day operations and supervision of the Society. In 1995, Cooke named Drain executive director of FCSI, while retaining the position of executive vice president.

Cooke was often involved in matters for other professional and trade organizations served by FSA; however, Drain's focus was purely on FCSI matters.

In late 2001, Cooke decided to step back from his strong involvement with FCSI. Continuing with FSA in other capacities,

Cooke, with enthusiastic FCSI Board approval, turned to his associate, naming Drain FCSI executive vice president.

"The transition was really smooth, as I had already developed a rapport with the Board," Drain says of the change. Taking over as executive vice president on January 1, 2002, Drain's service began during the unsettling aftermath of the September 11, 2001, terrorist attacks on the United States.

Drain plunged into the difficult task of organizing and coordinating FCSI's first conference as a worldwide organization in Barcelona in September 2002.

"I was very proud of the fact that we were able to pull that off so successfully just one year after 9/11," Drain says. The conference had two very important and symbolic outcomes. First, it gave confidence to the North Americans to come to the event, which was very well organized. Second, it was a highly visible proof to the Europeans and the rest of the membership that FCSI was truly a global Society.

The FCSI Europe Board of Trustees during the 1998 Conference in Malta. From left: Hugh Cade, Wolfgang Kanig, Ken Winch, Gerhard Kühnel, Alice Arnold, Barry Wells, Nicolas Elshof, and Jean-Pierre Grossi.

FCSI NORTH AMERICAN CHAIRS

2001–2002	George Zawacki
2002–2003	Rudy Miick
2003–2004	George Shockey
2004–2005	John Radchenko
2005–2006	Howard Stanford

Continuing Education

Starting in 2001, FCSI members moved significantly closer to certification as the Society successfully implemented a continuing education requirement. Professional members were expected to complete thirty approved continuing education units (CEUs) during a three-year period. FCSI staff would keep the official record which was made available to members for review at a secure website location available only by password.

The high-tech world of the internet website quickly added a number of professional membership functions for members. Among them were access to the FCSI Membership Directory, electronic voting for candidates to the Board, opinion polls, annual conference registration and postconference evaluation surveys, article archives, and webcasts of distance learning seminars.

A Change in the Length of Terms

Starting during the presidential term of Scott D. Legge in 2001, FCSI bylaws were changed, extending the president's term to two years instead of one. The scope of services provided by FCSI to its members, combined with the growing complexity of the role of the president and the Board of Directors, contributed to the membership's approval of the change. Many presidents voiced the frustration that the job was so multifaceted that by the time they were "up to speed" on the workings of the organization and their duties and responsibilities, it was already time to turn the gavel over to the next president.

By extending their terms to two years, the FCSI president was now able to spend a much more extended period of time governing from a position of strength and knowledge of the issues, the Society's inner workings, and familiarity with the membership which now numbered eleven hundred.

By the conclusion of 2002, FCSI's Board and staff had supervised a number of successful structural initiatives which were enhanced by the greater stability provided by the two-year officer term. As he left office, Scott Legge could point to these significant accomplishments: the formation of the long-planned and studied North American Division, the adoption of a completely rewritten and revised set of Articles of Incorporation and Bylaws, and the development of a new Code of Conduct.

Jean-Pierre Grossi of France and Sandra Matheson of Canada during a leadership summit meeting held before the 2002 conference

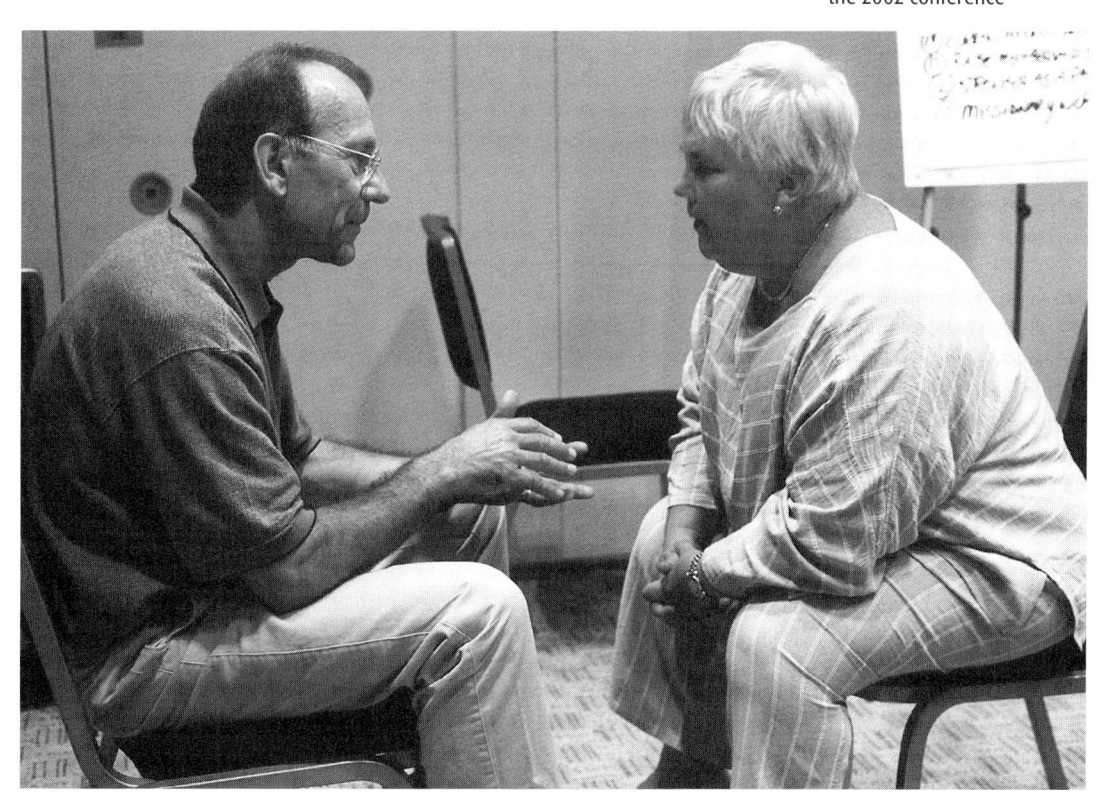

An International Village

A global perspective for FCSI permeated the Society as Al DaCosta assumed the presidency in September 2002. Fittingly taking on the mantle at the Annual Meeting in Barcelona, DaCosta's background gave him a particular advantage in understanding different cultures and bridging the gaps across the international village. DaCosta had lived and worked in Switzerland for several years and his multilingual abilities (Da Costa speaks five languages fluently) benefited the many members he visited during his term. DaCosta launched an extensive mission to visit FCSI chapters and local units around the world, making them each feel as valued, equal partners in the worldwide FCSI vision.

Another important change came about in November 2003, as the Board voted to create the North American Allied Member Board of Advisors (NAAMBA), a special committee composed of Allied Members. Former FCSI president Michael Colburn together with Keith R. Carpenter spearheaded the NAAMBA initiative. The group has been quite active in discussion and presenting issues important to Allied Members while at the same time giving a strong voice to their interest within the organization.

In 2003 and 2004, FCSI built upon the greater attention to structure and growing internationalization of the Society through expanded membership opportunities and greater attention to the programs and events taking place within the divisions worldwide.

It was a period of unprecedented international instability and disturbing trends towards international isolation and factionalism.

There have been countless periods in human history when the dynamic of diverse populations moved first in harmony, then into discord. Some say that conflict is the natural order.

However, as people and cultures clash, a constant among their interrelationships has always been the importance of understanding; awareness; information; and open, regular, and dispassionate communications. Maintaining all forms of communications develops familiarity, a basis upon which suspicions dissolve and cooperation flourishes.

Internationalization through open and regular communication is a clear strength of FCSI, which in a period of tension has flourished through understanding.

As FCSI approached its fiftieth anniversary celebration in 2005, one of the organization's greatest accomplishments has been the establishment of friendships, understanding, and a sense of common endeavor. It has formed a worldwide community of professional men and women who help each other in improving their individual services through greater awareness and understanding.

If only international political relationships could follow the lead of the eleven hundred members of the Foodservice Consultants Society International, the global community would be a far better, more peaceful place. It is something each member of the Society can take to heart and consider with deep pride. ■

50TH

… ANNIVERSARY

FCSI

1955-2005

"This is an organization of people well-respected by their peers…"

—Albert L. Da Costa, FCSI president 2002–2004

FCSI at Fifty

The half-century of FCSI existence has spanned tumultuous times in a period of significant cultural, political and economic change. As a tribute to the vision and drive of its founders, the organization has changed—and improved—during those years. Its resilience and success is due directly to the devotion and participation of the Society's members…

"It has been a wonderful experience!" says Kathleen Seelye, FCSI president in 1995–1996. Seelye reflects on her years of membership, service on the Board of Directors, and eventual terms as an officer of the Society during a period of great change and even greater growth.

"We had an opportunity to see tremendous change, tremendous growth and to feel like we were part of a very big movement forward," Seelye adds of that special time in the 1990s. "We worked together to make this a truly international Society."

"I am very pleased over the establishment of the European Division," says longtime European Division Executive Director Alice Arnold. She managed FCSI Europe affairs for years beginning in 1987 on a part-time basis. Arnold credits her company, SV-Service, and Bruno Brivio with supporting the FCSI Europe Division with office space and time as Arnold organized and supervised dozens of seminars in Europe. Through that period, Arnold has seen FCSI Europe grow from about 90 members in the late 1980s to more than 360 as the Society celebrates its fiftieth anniversary.

"We truly started from scratch," Arnold says of those early days when there was no organization, no office, no supplies, and no staff. However, today's FCSI Europe membership and activities have made the Society truly world-class.

Longtime FCSI member and former President James Little recalls the times when FCSI was a small group of colleagues and competitors who got together to "chew the fat."

"In the beginning, it was a bunch of good ol' boys and good ol' girls who'd gather around and chat," Little says of the days when meetings were much less formal. At times, discussions between members would become heated arguments, with few people paying attention to the invited speaker. "We're much more sophisticated now," Little adds.

Opposite: Members of the 2000 Conference Planning Committee and staff (from left, standing): Keith R. Carpenter, Ed Bernard, Marianne Luppold, Steve Carlson, Georgie Shockey, Woody Woodburn, Ken Schwartz. (From left, seated): Jackie Smith, Nadine Wilkerson, David Drain, Howard Stanford, Cindy Slone, Rosemary Osbourne.

COUNCIL OF FELLOWS

The Council of Fellows was created in 1981 as a means of recognizing extraordinary contributions by Society members to the industry, to the consulting profession and to FCSI.

Arthur C. Avery, FFCSI (1986)*

Ira B. Beer, FFCSI (1995)

John C. Birchfield Sr., FFCSI (2001)

Bruno M. Brivio, FFCSI (1999)

Hugh R. Cade, FFCSI (2002)

William J. Caruso, FFCSI (1986)

John C. Cini, FFCSI (1986)

Thomas Costello, FFCSI (2003)

Samuel Crabtree, FFCSI (1985)

William V. Eaton, FFCSI (1987)

Nicolas F. P. M. Elshof, FFCSI (2002)

John D. Fellers, FFCSI (1984)

Richard Flambert, FFCSI (1981)

Michael O. Johnson, FFCSI (2005)

Robert H. Kaiser, FFCSI (1983)

Tassos Kioulpapas, FFCSI (2001)

Ronald P. Kooser, FFCSI (1984)

George Kraft, FFCSI (1983)

Joseph W. Laschober, FFCSI (1988)

James H. Little, FFCSI (1985)

C. Russell Nickel, FFCSI (1984)

Robert E. Pacifico, FFCSI (2001)

Michael L. Pantano, FFCSI (2004)

Murray A. Perl, FFCSI (1985)

Benjamin Perlstein, FFCSI (1991)

Juan M. Prieto, A., FFCSI (1988)

Thomas D. Ricca, FFCSI (1997)

H. G. "Gene" Rice, FFCSI (1989)

Salvatore N. Romano, FFCSI (1993)

Fred Schmid, FFCSI (1981)

Kathleen H. Seelye, FFCSI (2001)

Leif Torné, FFCSI (2005)

Charles A. Wood, FFCSI (1983)

Beryl J. Yuhas, FFCSI (2001)

George G. Zipfel, FFCSI (1987)

Denotes year of induction into Council of Fellows

However, Little also sees that not everything has changed in the foodservice consultants' landscape. Echoing a common strain heard for decades within the profession, Little says that, "Probably the biggest challenge to the profession is trying to get the fees that are justified by the work we do." From time to time, and more often than anyone in the Society would care to admit, foodservice consultant fees get reduced, given low priority, or even eliminated, especially while working with and through third parties such as architects.

"Sometimes just getting paid is an issue," Little continues, detailing the fact that foodservice consultants are from time to time the last in line in a chain of professionals collaborating on a design project.

Immediate past president Al Da Costa sees many benefits to members, most of which are intangible yet of great intrinsic value. "FCSI's uniqueness is derived from the character of the people who became involved over the years," Da Costa says. "Involvement on the committee or Board level broadens one's horizons as individual contacts grow," Da Costa adds. "The opportunities to volunteer allow each member to benefit well beyond membership," Da Costa says. His is a tribute to the talented men and women who have stepped up to work at the many tasks resulting in great value to the international membership of the Society.

Robert Kaiser is one of the pioneers in the foodservice consulting profession. Kaiser is an FCSI Fellow and before that distinction was awarded to him, served a term as president of the ISFSC. Kaiser's specialty is operational consulting and over the years he has been a major factor in the recognition and acceptance of that particular "sub-niche" of foodservice consulting which at one time was primarily numbered with design consultants.

Phillip S. Cooke served as FCSI executive vice president from 1992 to 2001.

Today Kaiser sees that one of FCSI's greatest strengths includes the chance for consultants from differing disciplines to learn, work, and improve their own professional services through FCSI membership.

"There is a great opportunity for various consultants of differing backgrounds. The organization gives us a chance to interchange ideas and meet fellow professionals," Kaiser says. He is particularly proud and gratified by the significant increase in the number of operational consultants who have come into the field and have joined FCSI in recent years. "The design consultants have come to the conclusion that they can't be all things to all people," Kaiser adds.

"There is a great deal of interplay between the design consultants and the operational consultants," Kaiser continues. "That gives me a great amount of pride and I am very pleased to see it."

Former FCSI President William V. Eaton traces his association with the Society even before his career began officially. As a student at Cornell University, Eaton attended the prestigious School of Hotel Administration at the Ithaca, New York, college. That program had a

Beryl Yuhas served as FCSI president from 1997 to 1998. She died from cancer in August 2001, one month before her induction into the Council of Fellows. Her legacy lives on through her generous $100,000 donation to the FCSI Educational Foundation.

Michael Pantano served as FCSI president from 1999 to 2000.

HONOR ROLL OF PRESIDENTS

FFES/FFCS

1955–1958	Fred Schmid
1958–1960	Howard L. Post
1960–1962	Frank T. Hilliker
1962–1964	Arthur W. Dana
1964–1966	John Phillips
1966–1968	James Davidson
1968–1970	Carl Hansen
1970–1972	Keith Little
1972–1974	Samuel Crabtree
1974–1976	Robert C. Kline
1976–1977	Frank N. Giampietro
1977–1979	James H. Little

ISFSC

1958–1959	Harry Friedman
1959–1961	Richard Flambert
1961–1963	Donald Lundberg
1963–1965	Earl Triplett
1965–1967	John Fellers
1967–1969	George Zipfel
1969–1971	Arthur Avery
1971–1973	Wid O. Neibert
1973–1975	Joseph W. Laschober
1975–1976	C. Russell Nickel*
1976–1977	John C. Cini
1977–1978	Robert H. Kaiser

FCSI

1979–1980	William V. Eaton
1980–1981	Paul Hysen
1981–1982	Charles A. Wood
1982–1983	Ronald P. Kooser
1983–1984	Murray A. Perl
1984–1985	William J. Caruso
1985–1986	Stephen W. Marshall
1986–1987	Michael J. Stack
1987–1988	Michael G. Colburn
1988–1989	John C. Birchfield
1989–1990	Anthony A. Clevenger
1990–1991	Salvatore N. Romano
1991–1992	Thomas Costello
1992–1993	Carl W. Vail
1993–1994	Michael O. Johnson
1994–1995	Robert E. Pacifico
1995–1996	Kathleen H. Seelye
1996–1997	Brian T. Sill
1997–1998	Beryl J. Yuhas
1998–1999	Hugh R. Cade
1999–2000	Michael L. Pantano
2000–2002	Scott D. Legge
2002–2004	Albert Da Costa
2004–2006	Kenneth Winch

Starting in 1975, ISFSC presidents served one-year terms instead of the two-year terms held up until that time.

"Lunch 'n Learn" during the 2003 conference in New Orleans.

food facilities design course component pioneered and sponsored by the FFES.

"Before I graduated in 1961, I wrote a letter to each of the fifty-two members of FFES with my credentials, looking for a job," Eaton says with great pleasure about writing to the actual sponsors of the program he was enrolled in.

"Only two of them responded, and both indicated that I was overqualified to be on their staffs," Eaton related with a hearty laugh. But the story has a further unusual twist. According to Eaton, some months later one of the fifty-two firms he had written to but which had not replied, tracked Eaton down by calling the professor in charge of the program.

Eaton was offered a job with the firm and his career as a foodservice consulting professional was fully underway.

In later years, Eaton returned the favor by being involved in FFES/FFCS, participating loosely in the merger discussions, and serving his term immediately after the merger was approved, becoming the first president of FCSI. Following his presidential term, Eaton played a major role in the formation of and administration of the FCSI Educational Foundation.

"We initiated the fund with a fund-raising reception that cleared about $10,000-$15,000 through $25 ticket sales," Eaton says about the beginning of the charitable endeavor. Over the ensuing years, Eaton and the Foundation Board concentrated on raising enough money to make the foundation self-sustaining while finding a way to distribute meaningful awards to recipients.

"It's one of the most beneficial programs we have established and every year it gets better," Eaton says with obvious pride.

Eaton is also a clear supporter of testing and certification of FCSI members, a concept that has been discussed for years but which has eluded the Society. "Certainly, you cannot practice architecture unless you are recognized by the American Institute of Architects," Eaton says. "If it were similar for the foodservice consulting industry, the product that results from this would be better."

Hugh Cade

The silent auction during the 2000 conference in Washington, D.C. Proceeds benefit the FCSI Educational Foundation.

Executive Vice President David Drain sees the current challenge facing FCSI members as being one of promoting a higher awareness of the organization and its purpose.

"We are challenged with promoting the fact that professional foodservice consultants exist, that this organization exists, and that potential users of the services our members provide should choose an FCSI consultant," Drain says. "Our members have gone through a qualification process and potential clients can have confidence in choosing an FCSI consultant," Drain adds.

Drain says that one of the major initiatives he and the staff and membership are working on right now is the establishment of FCSI as a known brand that people can trust.

In addition to promoting the identity of the profession and the organization, Drain sees the immediate future as continuing in the path towards globalization. Although there is the constant drive towards increasing membership, it will not be done through any lowering of standards.

During a game show called "So You Think You Know About Foodservice?" at the Barcelona conference, teams had to guess types of beverages and from what countries the beverages originated.

Lourdes Labrador, Michael Pantano, and Yasuo Inoue.

"We will continue our focus on education and networking," Drain adds. "But we will be quantifying that through our continuing professional growth program."

The Foodservice Consultants Society International has traveled a great distance in time and perception since Fred Schmid gathered his colleagues and competitors in Chicago in 1955. The ancestor FFES began with fourteen charter members. Today FCSI boasts more than eleven hundred.

Along the way, the members, through volunteerism, hard work, dedication, and determination, have worked with staff leadership to build a worldwide organization of knowledge, information, and support.

And together, they have built a profession recognized around the globe. All this transpired in a mere fifty years. With that as background, just imagine what the next fifty will bring.

Above:
During the 2003 conference, Brian Maloney (left), his son Sean and FCSI Educational Foundation President Ed Norman present a check to the Children's Miracle Network. Sean Maloney, a cancer survivor, had benefited from the CMN years earlier.

Right:
The 2002–2003 European Board of Trustees (from left): Jean-Pierre Grossi, Urs von Allmen, Katia Daros, Gerhard Kuehnel, Alice Arnold, Rosemary Osbourne, Gerhard Franzen, Ken Winch, and Henk Kloosterhuis.

FCSI ANNUAL CONFERENCES

1955–1979–Chicago, Illinois
 (in conjunction with the NRA show)
1980–Miami, Florida
1981–Atlanta, Georgia
1982–Lake Tahoe, Nevada
1983–Dallas, Texas
1984–Toronto, Ontario
1985–New Orleans, Louisiana
1986–Paris, France (cancelled)
1987–Las Vegas, Nevada
1988–San Francisco, California
1989–Dallas, Texas
1990–New York, New York
1991–Atlanta, Georgia
1992–Phoenix, Arizona
1993–New Orleans, Louisiana
1994–San Antonio, Texas
1995–Las Vegas, Nevada
1996–Vancouver, British Columbia
1997–New Orleans, Louisiana
1998–Tucson, Arizona
1999–Dallas, Texas
2000–Washington, D.C.
2001–Orlando, Florida
2002–Barcelona, Spain
2003–New Orleans, Louisiana
2004–Toronto, Ontario
2005–Anaheim, California

European conferences

1987–Basel, Switzerland
1988–Düsseldorf, Germany
1989–Hamburg, Germany
1990–London, United Kingdom
1991–Amsterdam, The Netherlands
1992–London (January) and Paris
 (November)
1993–Basel, Switzerland
1994–Düsseldorf, Germany
1995–Milan, Italy
1996–No conference held;
 supported Vancouver conference
1997–Leipzig, Germany
1998–Malta
1999–Lyon, France
2000–Amsterdam, The Netherlands
2001–Capri, Italy
2002–No conference held;
 supported Barcelona conference
2003–Vienna, Austria
2004–No conference held;
 supported Toronto conference
2005–Berlin, Germany

Above:
Ken Sangster of Australia mans the FCSI booth during The NAFEM Show in 2003.

Right:
FCSI staffers Cindy Slone and Mary Gratzer flank member John Egnor.

Left:
FCSI Fellows (from left) Bob Pacifico, Hugh Cade, Tom Ricca, and Bruno Brivio, satired as Canadian Mounties, shared their wisdom in a pre-conference workshop at the 2004 conference in Toronto.

Below left:
FCSI Asia Pacific Chapter Chair Tim Smallwood.

Below:
FCSI Europe chairman Gerhard Kühnel and European Division administrator Sabine Wagner.

Right:
FCSI North America Chair-Elect Howard Stanford.

Below:
FCSI staff at the 2004 conference (left to right): Kevin Hall, Leigh Ann Kaufling, Travis Doster, Kelli Bailey, Cindy Slone, and David Drain.

Above:
2004 FCSI Conference Planning Committee (left to right): Sandra Matheson, Claudia Scotty, Dave Ek, Armando Pujatti, Karen Malody, Chris Bigelow, and Peggie Ulle.

Left:
FCSI North American Division Board members (left to right): John Radchenko, John Cornyn, Gary Lummis, Georgie Shockey, Ed Bernard, Howard Stanford, and Keith Carpenter.

Top:
Attendees at the 2000 conference.

Right:
At the FCSI Asia Pacific organizational meeting in Manila were (left to right) Phillip S. Cooke, Vivien Choi-Cheung, Imelda Silayan and Alburn William.

THE CONSULTANT AT LARGE by Wid Omar Neibert, FCSI

"When I told the mechanical people we needed negative pressure in here, I guess I should have quantified it."

Wid O. Neibert, a former ISFSC president, was an accomplished illustrator and contributed original cartoons to *The Consultant* for many years.

THE CONSULTANT

VOLUME XXII • NUMBER 1 • WINTER 1989

The Consultant

Volume XXV
Number 1
Winter 1992

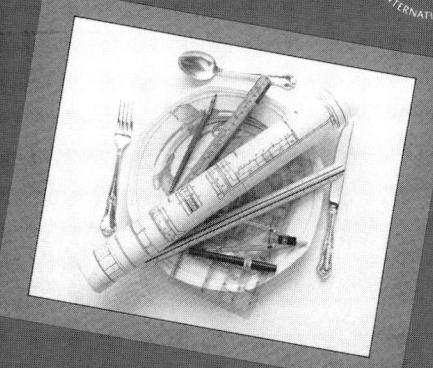

The CONSULTANT

A Quarterly Publication of Foodservice Consultants Society International

The Consultants' Forum

Putting Pizza Into a
Restaurant or Foodservice Facility

Developing a New Restaurant
Concept from Scratch:
A MAS Perspective

The Operator's Perspective:
Motorola's New Singapore Facility

SULTANT
VOLUME 26, NUMBER 1

- ...g Face of Correctional Foodservice
- ...arket Perspectives - A New Feature
- ...nual Seminar Report
- ...rough Communication

Volume 27, Number 1

...NT
...ulting

THE CONSULTANT
VOLUME XXV • NUMBER 3

In This Issue:

Meet the New FCSI Staff

From The FCSI Chicago Seminar:
- Phillip S. Cooke on Industry Trends
- Tom Costello and Foodservice Editors On the New Realities
- Presidents' Panel on Challenges & Changes Ahead for Non-Commercial Foodservice

Is Smart Heat Smart Equipment?

Computer Update

...the Montreal Protocol

---

the consultant
A PUBLICATION OF THE FOODSERVICE CONSULTANTS SOCIETY INTERNATIONAL, SECOND QUARTER 2004, VOL. 37, NUMBER 2

- Athens Foodservice Prepares for the Games
- FCSI Annual Conference Preview
- Also: What's Hot in Toronto
- Excellence in Design: Correctional Services in Ontario
- The 10 Commandments of Service Design

ABOUT THE AUTHOR

Foodservice Consultants Society International: 50 Years of Service, 1955–2005 is the fifty-first book written by popular author and historian Robert R. Morris. He specializes in researching and writing organizational and institutional histories. Several of the photos in this book are his original photography.

A former teacher, Morris has concentrated on history writing for more than twenty years. When not writing, he spends considerable time working with nonprofit charitable organizations in the Chicago area.

Morris and his wife live in northeastern Illinois.